Maths Games

Addition and
Subtraction Games

Sue Atkinson

HOPSCOTCH
EDUCATIONAL PUBLISHING

CONTENTS

Published by
Hopscotch Educational Publishing Ltd.,
Unit 2, The Old Brushworks, 56 Pickwick Road,
Corsham, Wiltshire SN13 9BX
Tel: 01249 701701

© 2003 Hopscotch Educational Publishing

Written by Sue Atkinson
Series design Blade Communications
Illustrated by Susan Hutchison
Printed by Clintplan Limited, Southam

ISBN 1-904307-46-9

Sue Atkinson hereby asserts her moral right to be identified as the author of this work in accordance with the Copyright, Designs and Patents Act, 1988.

The author would like to thank the many teachers and children from the following schools who trialled these activities:

Bishop Perrin Primary School, Richmond

Sheen Mount Primary School, Richmond

Upton House School, Windsor

Kinsale Middle School, Hellesdon, Norwich

Eye Primary School, Peterborough

Happisburgh First School, Norfolk

Aslacton Primary School, Norfolk

Alpington Primary School, Norfolk

Scarning Primary School, Dereham, Norfolk

West Thurrock Primary School, Essex

St Josephs Primary School, Stanford-le-Hope, Essex

Maths games have been shown to have a positive influence on children's learning and this series of books is designed to raise achievement in your class.

This book of games is suitable for children who are:
- working on learning objectives from the early learning goals to about level 3;
- lower achievers in Key Stages 2 and 3. (The artwork has been designed to be suitable for use with older children);
- in need of more practice with certain key objectives in the National Numeracy Framework.

Using the games

The games are clearly differentiated and are suitable for:

- the whole class to play at the same time;
- working independently in group-work time;
- working with other adults in the classroom;
- use at home as homework or borrowed as part of a maths games library.

It is important to refer to the objectives for the other year groups to give your groups/class a range of differentiated games.

The structure of the book

The chart/contents list on page 5 shows the main learning objective for each of the games.

Each game has a double page of teacher notes followed by photocopiable game boards and/or cards specific to that game. Any resource that is needed for more than one of the games is called a generic sheet; these are at the back of the book.

Also at the back of the book are the rules of the games, presented in such as way that they can be cut out, mounted onto card and used by the children. See page 4 for more information on the rules.

The structure of the teacher's notes

These show the main learning objective, the resources required, how to play the game, variations for the different age ranges and ideas for the plenary session.

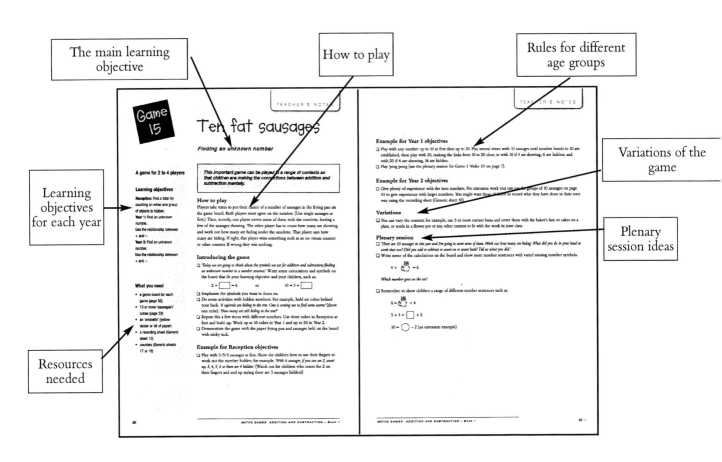

The main learning objective

How to play

Rules for different age groups

Learning objectives for each year

Resources needed

Variations of the game

Plenary session ideas

Preparing the games

The teacher's notes will tell you what you need to play the games and which pages you need to photocopy. You can copy the game boards onto card if you want, or onto paper and laminate them.

The photocopiable number cards, spinners and counters are best copied onto card before they are cut for ease of handling them.

Using the spinners

When you cut out each spinner, cut out the rectangle of card that it is drawn on because having this to hold makes spinning the paper-clip easier.

With one hand, trap the paper-clip with the pencil in the middle of the spinner. Flick the paper-clip around with a finger on the other hand. If the clip stops on a line, that player can decide which of the two sections he or she wants.

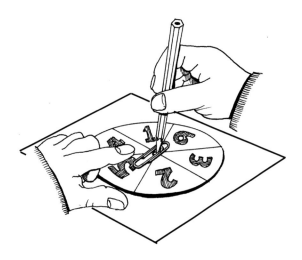

Rules for the games

Rules for the games are explained in the teacher's notes. At the back of the book the rules are presented in such a way that they can be cut out, mounted onto card and used by the children. Some of the games have two versions of the rules. Some of the rules contain blank boxes for the teacher to complete with the relevant numbers to be used in the game. There is a blank rules card which can be used for variations of the games. You might find it helpful for a games library always to stick a copy of the rules on the back of each game, as well as a copy of the rules that can be referred to as the game is played.

Storing the games

Store the games in plastic folders that have been labelled to show the title of the game, the learning objective and the contents of the folder (for example '1 game board, 2 spinners, rules, 4 counters').

A final note

Above all, boost children's self-esteem by your focused assessment questions and your praise and encouragement, so that maths is enjoyed by everyone.

Linking maths concepts to the games in this book

Games	1	2	3	4	5	6	7	8	9	10	11	12	13	14	15	16	17	18	19	20
Understanding addition and subtraction																				
Use the vocabulary involved in + and –	✓	✓	✓	✓	✓	✓	✓	✓	✓	✓	✓	✓	✓	✓	✓	✓	✓	✓	✓	✓
Begin to relate addition to combining two groups of objects	✓			✓						✓							✓			
Begin to recognise that more than two numbers can be added							✓										✓			
Begin to relate subtraction to 'taking away' and 'difference'		✓	✓		✓	✓														
Understand the operation of + and – /use the +, – and = signs		✓	✓								✓			✓	✓				✓	
Understand that subtraction is the inverse of addition		✓	✓		✓	✓								✓	✓	✓				
Find one more or one less than a number				✓						✓	✓									
Adding 2 two-digit numbers																		✓		
Finding difference and counting up from smaller to larger number						✓								✓			✓			
Find a total by counting when one group of objects is hidden															✓	✓	✓			
Partition a given number of objects into two groups									✓		✓	✓	✓							
Rapid recall of addition and subtraction facts																				
Know by heart all pairs of numbers with a total of 10/20/multiples of 10	✓																			
Addition facts for small numbers and corresponding subtraction facts	✓												✓							
Mental calculation strategies + and –																				
Add a pair of numbers (then three) mentally to 10 and then 20	✓		✓	✓			✓	✓	✓								✓	✓		
Use knowledge that addition can be done in any order to do mental calculations more efficiently							✓	✓	✓				✓					✓		
Putting the larger number first and counting on in ones							✓	✓												
State the subtraction corresponding to a given addition and vice versa		✓																✓		
Identify doubles and near doubles										✓										
Add and subtract 9 or 11 by adding 10 then adding or subtracting one												✓								
Solving problems																				
Use developing mathematical ideas to solve practical problems																	✓	✓	✓	✓
Consolidation and assessment																				✓

Make 10

Learning number bonds to 10 (and 20)

A game for two to four players

Learning objectives

Reception: Begin to use the vocabulary involved in adding and subtracting.
Begin to relate addition to combining two groups of objects.

Year 1: Know by heart all numbers with a total of 10.

Year 2: Know by heart all addition and subtraction facts to at least 10; all pairs of numbers with a total of 20; all pairs of multiples of 10 with a total of 100.

What you need

- cubes/teddies/counters
- number cards (Generic sheets 1–4) or fish cards (Generic sheets 5 and 6)
- a thick red felt-tipped pen

> This game can be played at many different levels. It covers a most important learning objective and is a game to play frequently during mental maths time (see the whole class game in the Plenary session).

How to play

The aim of the game is to be able to pick up the correct card from the table to make number partners. So, if you are making partners of 10, to find red 7 you must pick up black 3. If you are right, you keep the card and at the end, see who has the most cards. To extend the length of the game you can use more than one set of cards.

Note for the teacher

On the back of each number card, write in red the number that, when added to that on the reverse, will total 10 (or whichever target total number you are working with.) So, if your target total number is 10, on the back of the 6 number card you will write 4 using a thick red felt-tipped pen. If your target total is 20, write on the back of the 6 number card in red the number 14.

Introducing the game

❏ Say to the children *'Today we are going to find the number partners for 10. Hold up ten fingers. Now fold down four of them. How many are left standing up?'*

❏ *'Make a cube train of 10, but in two different colours so you could have 6 blue and 4 red. 6 and 4 are number partners of 10.'*

Example for Year 1 objectives

❏ Place the cards on a table, black numbers facing up. The children take turns to say the number they are going to find; for example, *'I am going to find the red 8.'* That child picks the card with the black 2 and shows all the others the red 8. She wins a counter or keeps the card.

❏ Use cards to 20 before the end of the year.

Example for Reception objectives

❏ You could play this with numbers written on the blank fish cards (Generic sheet 5) without writing numbers on the back, so that the children can see both of the numbers at the same time. They have to find two cards that make the total you have asked them for. If they use two fish to make 5, for example, only use about four sets of the number cards 1–4. When you first play the game make sure you do plenty of work with fingers and cubes or teddies so that the children are seeing addition as combining two groups of objects.

❏ Move on to making number bonds of 10 as soon as you can. (See the Year 1 example.)

❏ *'Hold up 3 fingers. How many are folded down?' (7) 'So you need a 7 to go with your 3.'*

❏ Or play the game as for Pelmanism with the cards face down. Players take turns to turn over two cards. If the pair of numbers make 10, for example 3 and 7, they keep that pair. If they don't make 10, the cards are returned face down to exactly the same place.

❏ An even easier game, and one that will encourage counting, is to use the dotty fish cards (Generic sheet 6). Note that you might want to make a fish with no dots from the blank fish on Generic sheet 5.

Example for Year 2 objectives

❏ Play as for Year 1 with cards to 20 (ie black 17 has a red 3 on the back). Show the children how cards to 20 link to cards to 10. For example, on the cards to 10, the black 7 has a red 3 on the back, and with cards to 20, the black 7 has a red 13 on the back.

Variations

❏ A harder game is to choose another number to make pairs, for example to 15. So black 7 would have red 8 on the back and so on.

❏ Challenge the children to make their own game. Give them a number to suit their experience, such as 17, and ask them to make fish cards to play the game to 17. The children can challenge each other, for example, *'Find red 14.'*

Plenary session

❏ *'Show me how you can use your fingers to work out the number partners for 10.'*

❏ *'Let's play "Ping pong" to 10. (A whole class mental maths game.) If I say 7 you must answer 3. If I say ping, you say pong. If I say 5 you must say 5 because 5 and 5 makes 10.'*

❏ *'How do you know that 4 is the right number to go with 10? How could you check your answer?'*

❏ Make a large version of Spinner 1 (10 sections) on Generic sheet 7 (see the introduction for how to make up the spinners). Put the spinner on the floor and use it to generate the numbers 0–9. You call out the number you spin and the class has to call out the number that makes it up to 10 (or 20). So, if you spin zero, the children have to shout out 10.

❏ Use a range of words for addition and help the children to say number sentences; for example, *'4 add 6 makes 10 altogether.'*

❏ *'Show me how you can use your fingers to show why 4 goes with 6.'*

❏ *'If 8 is the number partner of 2, what would you put with 2 if we were trying to make 20?'*

❏ *'Tell me about this number pattern I'm writing on the board.'* (Write up 9 + 1 = 10, 8 + 2 = 10 and so on.) *'What would come next? How do you know?'*

Game 2

Snakey sentences

Using the vocabulary of addition and subtraction

A game for two to six players

Learning objectives

Reception: Begin to use the vocabulary involved in adding and subtracting.

Year 1: Understand the operations of addition and subtraction (as 'take away' and 'difference') and use the related vocabulary.

Year 2: Use and begin to read the vocabulary of addition and subtraction; use the +, – and = signs.

What you need

- sets of 1–9 number cards (Generic sheet 1)
- the snakes sheet (page 10)
- maths word cards (Generic sheet 14)
- cubes
- a recording sheet (Generic sheet 10)
- Generic sheet 17 (Score a goal)

This game needs to be supervised at first. When children are able to play it independently, you will need to be available to sort out any disputes.

How to play

The idea of the game is to make snake sentences on the snakes sheet on page 10, using at least one of the snake words from Generic sheet 14.

Each player needs a snake sheet. Give each player one snake word and in turns they make up a number sentence with their word in it. For example, given the word 'add' a child might say '2 add 2 makes 4.' That is correct so she puts the word 'add' on her first snake. Then the next child uses a word. Everyone tries to have a different word on each snake by the end. When you are supervising the group you can control which words are given to each child, ensuring that they get a selection of words, and you can choose words that the children know in order to to boost their confidence. When they are playing independently, you can start by each child being dealt five words, or place them all face down and they take turns to pick one. If a child picks up a card already on one of their snakes, that child misses that turn.

Introducing the game

❑ Say to the children *'Today we are going to think very carefully about some of the words that we use when we are adding and subtracting. Can anyone tell me a word that we use?'* Write the words the children know on the board and teach them the ones that they don't know that are on the word sheet.

Example for Reception objectives

❑ If you keep this game to a supervised activity you can restrict the number of words you use, starting with just the basic ones. You can pick a word and ask each child to make a different number sentence, using their fingers/cubes/farm animals. For example, if the word 'take away' is used, one child might say *'If the farmer has 3 sheep in the field then he takes one of them away to the barn, there will only be 2 left in the field.'* The next child might talk about currant buns in the shop and how many are taken away.

Example for Year 1 objectives

❏ Play as above, at first with the words face up to make the game easier. A good reader in each group would be helpful. Keep an eye on the game and, if you can, sit with the group for a few minutes asking them to tell you their sentences.

Example for Year 2 objectives

❏ These children can use the snakes to record their complete sentence in writing. If you laminate the board, the writing can just be wiped off. (Or use the recording sheet on Generic sheet 10.) Encourage children to write complete sentences as well as using the +, – and = signs. You could challenge groups to work together to see how many different number sentences they can write.

Variations

❏ Pairs of children can play this game using the board on Generic sheet 17 (Score a goal). They place their counters on the two centre spaces and move a space towards the goal each time they are successful. Remind them that when a word is picked, they must say a complete number sentence.

❏ Vary the game a little by putting words onto large copies of a spinner, such as Spinner 2, 4 or 7 (Generic sheets 7 and 8). Each player spins a word in turn. This game has more luck in it.

❏ To write the rules for the children to read for these variations of the game, use the blank rules on page 96.

Plenary session

❏ *'Did you learn any new words today?'*

❏ *'Which words did we use that mean take away?'*

❏ *'If you had to make a sixth snake sentence what could you say?'*

❏ *'What does this sign (=) mean? Which words can you use for =?'*

❏ *'Put some numbers into this sentence:*

   '4 is 2 more than ?'

   '3 is 2 fewer than ?'

   '? is 4 fewer than ?'

❏ *'The difference between ? and ? is 2'*

❏ You might want to build up a class poster of words used for addition and subtraction that you can refer to every day for a month in mental maths time.

Recording sheet

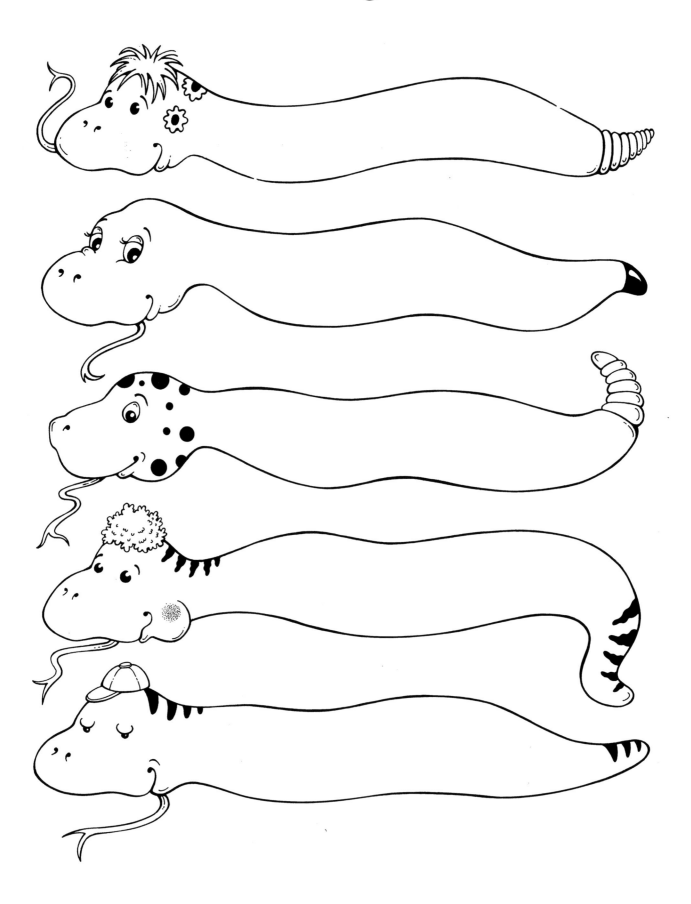

Game 3

Three blind mice

Understanding that subtraction is the inverse of addition

A game for two or more players

Learning objectives

Reception: Begin to understand how addition and subtraction are linked, and use the appropriate vocabulary.
Year 1: Understand the operations of addition and subtraction and use the related vocabulary.
Year 2: Understand that subtraction is the inverse of addition.

What you need

- cubes/teddies
- mice number cards (page 13)
- blank mice cards (page 14)
- a recording sheet (Generic sheet 10)
- number lines (Generic sheet 11)
- maths word cards (Generic sheet 14)

> This game needs supervision at first. When children start to play it independently, you will need to be on hand to sort out disputes and check that they understand what they are doing.

How to play

The idea of the game is to find three blind mice that 'go together' and make a number sentence that everyone agrees is right. Mice cards are placed face down individually on the table. Players take it in turns to take three cards. If the cards 'go together' the player keeps them and tells the others a number sentence that can be made with them. For example, if 2, 4 and 6 are turned over, that player could say '6 take away 2 leaves 4.' If the numbers don't go together to make a sentence, the cards must be replaced in exactly the same position that they were in. So if 7 and 6 are picked with 2, the numbers don't go together (but see extension in Year 2). When there are only a few cards left face down on the table it is much more satisfying to decide to stop, count up the scores for each person and start another game. The winner is the player with the most sets of cards.

Notes for the teacher

Prepare sets of mice number cards, about three sets of three numbers for each child playing in a group of four, ie about 36 cards. Choose mice numbers to suit your children such as 1–10 or use the blanks on page 14 to make larger numbers. You need to include several copies of the lower numbers, such as 1–4, and just one each of the numbers above 6.

Introducing the game

- ❏ Say to the children *'This game will help you to see how addition undoes subtraction, and subtraction undoes addition. Hold up four fingers. Now add one more. How many now? Now fold that one finger down again. How many now? You added one to four and got five, then you took it away again and got back to four again!'*
- ❏ Repeat this kind of activity in several different contexts; for example, start with a 'train' of 10 cubes, take away 3 then add them on again, and so on.
- ❏ *'If you add on a number, then take it away again, you get back to the number you first started with. If I gave Tom 3 apples then gave him one more, how many would he have? What if he gave me back that one apple?'*
- ❏ When the children are ready for number sentences, write on the board words and/or symbols sentences such as 3 and 4 more makes 7; 7 take away 3 leaves 4. Make sure you support every number sentence with cubes/fingers/number lines and show how you can make lots of number sentences with those same three numbers.

Example for Reception objectives

❏ Prepare several sets of 1–4 number cards, two each of 5, 6 and 7 and just one each of the 8–10 cards (but have some spare available). Play the game as a supervised activity with cubes/mice focusing on the children developing their vocabulary. Keep the mice cards face up and help the children to select three cards that go together. Supervise each child using apparatus or fingers to illustrate their three blind mice numbers.

❏ Encourage them to say their sentences out loud. *'I can make 2 add 1 makes 3 altogether, and I can make 3 take away 1 leaves 2.'* Try to make the point that taking away and then adding back again gets you back to your first number, so adding and subtracting are the opposite of each other.

Example for Year 1 objectives

❏ Prepare several sets of 1–6 cards and just a few 7–10 cards. (But see the extension using blanks in Year 2.) Play the game with the cards face down. As the focus of the activity is on linking particular numbers, you don't need to use numbers beyond 10 at first. Let the children bring around two of their sets of cards to the plenary session to tell you their sentences.

Example for Year 2 objectives

❏ Make it clear which numbers you have used on the mice; for example, up to 10 or 12.

❏ Extend the game by having some blank mice cards available for making a third number for when the other two numbers need a number larger than the set being used. So, if the set of cards being played with just goes up to 10 and 5, 8 and 1 are picked up. The player can choose to discard one card, for example the 1, and make their own number for the third card. 8 add 5 is 13 so the child takes a blank mouse card and writes '13' on it and keeps that set of three cards.

❏ Focus on subtraction being the inverse of addition by asking each child to say two related number sentences each time, one for addition and one for subtraction. You might want them to record their sentences on Generic sheet 10 to bring to the plenary.

Variations

❏ Give pairs of children some blank mice and some maths word cards from Generic sheet 14. Ask them to cut and stick number sentences using just the same three numbers each time. They could try to see who could make the most different number sentences. (So, '5 subtract 1 is 4' is different from '5 – 1 = 4'.) This can work as a whole class activity in Year 2.

Plenary session

❏ When the children tell you their number sentences, challenge them each time to make two more sentences with those numbers, but using different words, one for addition and one for subtraction.

❏ Make the link to addition and counting on (and subtraction and counting back) by showing how the number sentences can be made on a floor or wall number line/track. *'Stand on 4 and count on 2. You land on 6. Now step back 2. You get back to 4 where you started! So counting on and counting back are the opposite of each other!'*

❏ Ask selected children to come to the front and select (from face-up cards) three numbers that go together. Be ready for those children that haven't yet grasped the point! It is quite a complex concept.

❏ *'Explain why 5, 2 and 4 don't go together.'*

❏ *'What is a third mouse number that we need to go with 6 and 4?'* (It could be 2 or 10.)

❏ With a large copy of the maths words (Generic sheet 14) and the mice you could make up number sentences and put them on display for a few weeks.

Number cards

Blank number cards

Something fishy

Adding numbers mentally

A game for two or more players

Learning objectives

Reception: Counting – begin to relate addition to combining two groups of objects. (Find one more or one less from 1–10.)

Year 1: Add a pair of numbers mentally to 10 and then 20. (Find one or ten more or less than a number 0-30.)

Year 2: Adding numbers mentally – use knowledge that addition can be done in any order to do mental calculations more efficiently; for example, make 10s.

What you need

- fish dotty cards and blanks (Generic sheets 5 and 6)
- garden sticks or long bits of plastic Meccano
- string, paper-clips and a horseshoe magnet
- a 'pond' (a container) or a bag for older children
- counters from Generic sheets 18 and 19
- number lines/track (Generic sheets 11–13)

> This game can be used for basic counting of dots and can be extended to addition of 2 or 3 numbers at any level.

How to play

Players take turns to fish out two fish with a magnetic fishing rod and add the numbers on the fish together. If they are right, they win a fishy counter from Generic sheet 18 and then put the numbered fish back in the pond and give them a stir around. You could cut out around the fish but the game works just as well if they are left as rectangles. Put a paper clip on the 'nose' of each fish and put them in the pond. Make a fishing rod with the string and magnet.

Notes for the teacher

Prepare the fish cards from Generic sheets 5 and 6 to suit your children. For example, for Reception children you might have fish numbered 1 to 5 and for Year 2 by the end of the summer term you might have two two-digit numbers.

Introducing the game

❑ Say to the children *'Today we are going to add two numbers together. Hold up three fingers on one hand and two on the other. How many fingers altogether? Now pick up five cubes and then another two. How many altogether?'*

Example for Reception objectives

❑ Use the dotty fish cards. At first you can adapt the game just to recognising and counting the dots on one fish and asking the child to make a cube train with that number of cubes. With the blank fish on Generic sheet 5 you could make more dotty fish but make the dots random so that they need to be counted. (However, it is important for children to recognise quickly the dice/domino/doubles patterns to 10 as this can help to develop visual images of numbers.)

Example for Year 1 objectives

❑ Number the blank fish from 1–10 so that the children have to do additions such as 5 + 9 and so on. Support this with either a blank number line (Generic sheet 11) or the number line to 20 (Generic sheet 12). Later in the year move on to include the numbers 11–15, and with some children you could include up to 20. You might want to support this more difficult addition with the number track to 100 on Generic sheet 13 or the blank number lines on Generic sheet 11.

Example for Year 2 objectives

❏ You can adapt the game by using a bag as a pond and using any numbers on the blank fish or use number cards (Generic sheets 1–4).

❏ You can also use the fish to add three numbers.

❏ To add three numbers when two of them total 10, put fish numbered 12–30 in the pond and have a bag with the number cards 0–10 and a further set of cards 0–10 face up. Players take turns to take a larger number fish from the pond, such as 17, then a card from 1 to 10 from the bag, such as 4, and they have to select a third number from the face up cards, in this case a 6. So with 17 on the fish, 4 and 6, they can record: $17 + 4 + 6 = 17+10 = 27$.

Variations

❏ For Years 1 and 2 children you can have two ponds (bags), one with fish numbered above 11 and the other with lower numbers such as 2–6. Players take one fish with a small number then another with a larger number. They tell their partner what they are doing as they put the larger number first, for example 17, then add on the lower number. If they add correctly, putting the larger number first, they win a fish counter and/or show their calculation on a blank number line (Generic sheet 11).

❏ You can make a game about finding one more or one less from the numbers 1–10 by making a set of 1–10 fish cards and playing as above but with this different learning objective. Children take turns to fish, look at their number and have to say what is one more. If they are correct they win a counter.

❏ Similarly, you can use fish or number cards 10–30 and the player has to say what is 10 more or 10 less. Alternatively, use the 10–100 number cards in 10s (Generic sheets 1–4) and say what is 100 more.

❏ To write the rules for the children to read for these variations of the game, use the blank rules on page 96.

Plenary session

❏ *'When you have three fingers on one hand and five on the other, how many do you have altogether?'*

❏ *'Take some green cubes and some blue ones. Show me how many you have. Now put them together. How many altogether? Now make an adding sentence with your two numbers. Now take away the blue cubes. How many are left?'*

❏ *'When you add two numbers together, do you end up with a larger number altogether?'*

❏ *'Make a cube train of ten cubes/make a line of six teddies. Now take some away. How many are left?'*

Game 5

Feed the penguins

Understanding and using the language of subtraction (and linking subtraction and addition)

A game for two to four players

> This game can be used just with 'taking away' at first and you might find that to use the word 'difference' effectively you need to supervise the game. This game can also introduce zero as 'none left'.

Learning objectives

Reception: Using the language of subtraction (take away).

Year 1: Understanding and using the language of subtraction as 'taking away' and 'difference'.

Year 2: Using the language of addition and subtraction. Understanding that subtraction is the inverse of addition.

What you need

- pebbles, cubes or teddies
- a game board for each group (page 19 or 20)
- a counter each
- lots of 'fish' counters (Generic sheet 18) or cubes
- a 1–6 dice or spinner (Generic sheet 7)
- number lines to 20 (Generic sheet 12)
- a recording sheet (Generic sheet 10)

How to play

Each player starts by counting out 20 'fish' counters (Generic sheet 18) or cubes – an opportunity to assess counting to 20. (For a teacher-independent game have the 'fish' ready before the lesson.) Players take turns to throw the dice or spin the spinner and move that many spaces around the penguin pool. If they land on a space with fish in it, they feed that many of their cubes/fish to the penguins by counting them and removing them from their cube trains or pile of fish. These can be put in the pool in the middle of the board or, when there are more than two players, discarded into a box so that they go out of play. When you are able to supervise the game, encourage each child to make a number sentence each time; for example, *I had 20 cubes and I had to take away 2 so now I have 18 left.* Encourage the children to count back on a number line each time rather than counting all 18 cubes in 1s from 1! The winner is the first player to feed all their fish to the penguins, or the player with the fewest fish after going once round the board.

Introducing the game

❏ Say to the children *Today we are going to play a subtraction game so that you will learn more about taking away.'* Give, or ask the children to count out, a few pebbles/cubes/teddies to each child and ask them to count them. Then give an instruction such as *'Take away 2'* asking the children how many they have left each time. Make sentences; for example, *I had 16 teddies and I took away 3 so now I have 13 left.'* With less experienced children stick to just five or six objects at first until they are quite sure about what 'take away' means. Explain about penguin feeding time at the wildlife park or the zoo.

Example for Reception objectives

❏ Prepare enough '20 trains' or pile of fish for each child. Show them how to match one fish on the board for each one of their fish to be fed to the penguins. You could use the blank Spinner 4 from Generic sheet 7 and mark it with just 1, 2 or 3 to keep the steps along the track small. Saying a number sentence each time can be just *'I'm taking away 2 fish'.* Unless you are there, saying how many left each time might be too demanding. The winner can be determined as the player with the shortest '20 train' or least fish at the end, or the first player to have none left in order to introduce zero.

Example for Year 1 objectives

❑ These play the same as for the Reception game but encourage them to say a number sentence each time. Play just once around the board and the winner is the player with the fewest fish left, but only if they can say what the difference is between their fish and all the other players by putting their cube trains together. For example, *'I have 4 left and Jake has 6 left and the difference between 4 and 6 is 2.'*

❑ For a teacher-independent game ask the children to bring their left-over fish to the plenary session where you can show them how to work out the difference. If it is likely that there will be time for more than one game, players need to keep their left-over fish carefully at the end of each game.

Example for Year 2 objectives

❑ Play as before but ask each child to record their work on the recording sheet (Generic sheet 10). You can use much larger numbers using one of the blank spinners and the blank track on page 20. For this you will need to draw in the quantities of fish you want the children to work with.

❑ To include addition, use the buckets on the track to add some more fish. For example, each bucket could have a number in it, or you can make a rule that landing on a bucket means collect 5 more fish. This will make the number sentences involve addition as well as subtraction. For example, *'I had 13 fish left but then I added 10 so now I have 23 fish altogether.'*

Variations

❑ The game can be played as an addition game picking up 'fish' instead of taking them away.
❑ Landing on the bucket can mean you get an extra go.
❑ Play with a spinner with much larger numbers on the spinner and draw in more fish on the board.
❑ Use the blank track game (page 20) for children to make up their own rules.
❑ To write the rules for the children to read for these variations of the game, use the blank rules on page 96.

Plenary session

❑ *'I started with some fish in my bucket and when I fed 2 of them to the penguins I had 11 left. How many did I have in my bucket before I took away the two?'*
❑ *'8 take away 2 is 6. What other subtraction sentence can you make with 8, 2 and 6?'*
❑ *'Alice ended up with these 5 cubes and Dara ended up with 7 cubes. Someone come and show me how to put their cubes side by side to show the difference between 5 and 7.'*
❑ *'Alice is 6 and her little brother is 4. What is the difference in their ages?'*
❑ *'Peter penguin ate 7 fish and Pauline penguin ate 10 fish. What is the difference between 7 and 10? How did you work it out?'*
❑ *'Someone make a number sentence with the word "difference" in it.'*
❑ *'When you take away 2 and then add 2 back on, what happens?' (You end up with the number you started with.) 'Someone make me a sentence where you take some away first but then you add the same number back on.'*
❑ *'Now make a sentence where you take some away then add a different number back on.'*
❑ *'What is 10 add 2 take away 2?'*
❑ *'What can you tell me about addition and how it is linked to subtraction?'*

Game board 1

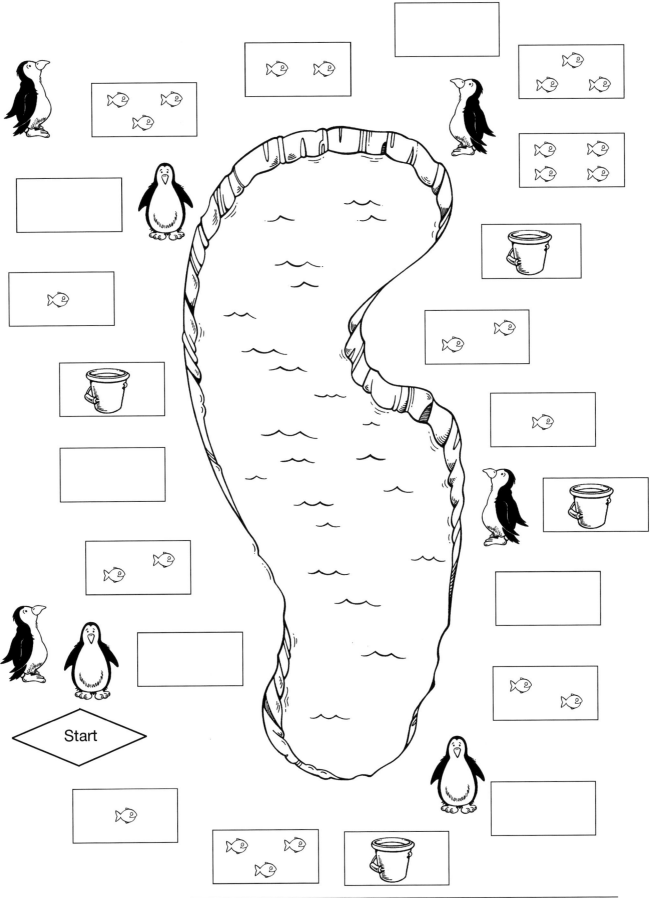

Game board 2

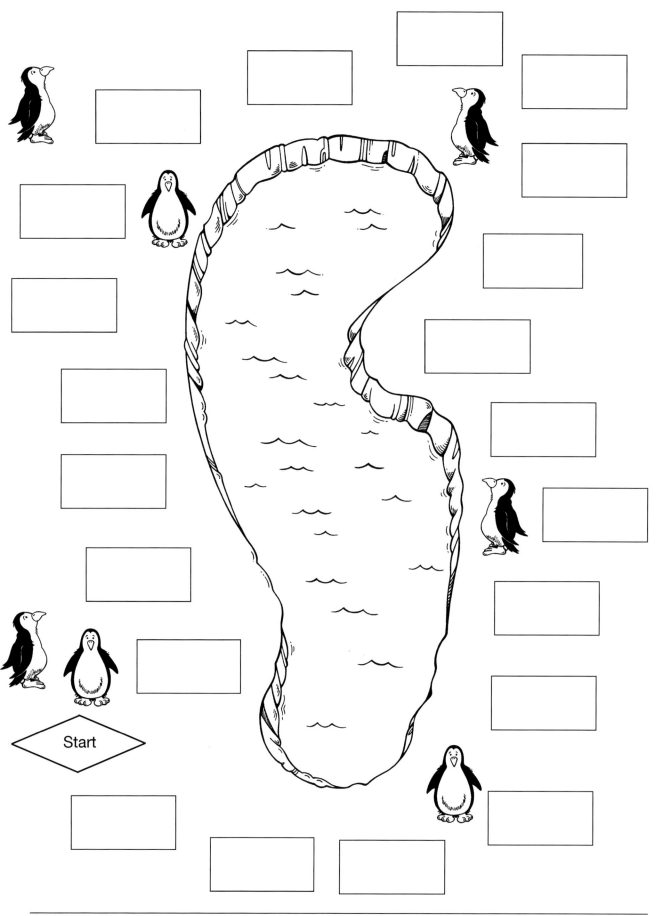

Game 6

Difference pairs

Finding differences and counting up from the smaller number to the larger

A game for two to eight players

A game for two to eight players

Learning objectives

Reception: Comparing two numbers and saying which one is more. Adding/subtracting 1 to a number.
Year 1: Understanding subtraction as 'difference'.
Year 2: Finding a small difference by counting up from the smaller number to the larger.

What you need

- number cards (Generic sheets 1–4)
- dotty cards (Generic sheet 15)
- a large number line and 100 square
- cubes
- a number line to 20 (Generic sheet 12)
- blank number lines (Generic sheet 11)

Children sometimes find 'difference' a difficult concept and need support to link it to subtraction and to counting up from the smaller number to the larger.

How to play

Cards are laid face down on the table and players take turns to turn over 2 cards. If they have a difference of 1 (or 2, decide on the rules before you start) the player keeps that pair. If they don't have the correct difference, the cards are put back in exactly the same place. You can extend the game so that children have to make a number sentence with their cards; for example, *'I've got 5 and 3 and they have a difference of 2'*, or *'the difference between 5 and 3 is 2.'*

Introducing the game

❏ Say to the children *'Today we are going to learn about the difference between two numbers, finding cards that are 1 (or 2) more than the other one.'*
❏ *'Hold up 5 fingers. On the other hand hold up 4 fingers. Which is more, 4 or 5? What is the difference between 4 and 5? Tell me some other numbers that have a difference of one. Now tell me some numbers that have a difference of 2.'*
❏ Make some cube trains with a difference of 2. Let the children investigate this in groups. Try to establish that a difference of 2 can work with any numbers, for example 98 and 100. Demonstrate these differences on a number line as well as on a hundred square. Show how to draw a step of 2 on a number line.

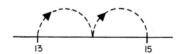

'The difference between 13 and 15 is 2.'

Example for Year 1 objectives

❏ Children can play with two sets of cards, 1–10 at first, and find a pair with a difference of 1. Extend the game with the 'teen' number cards. You can ask the children to show their two numbers on a number line to 20 (Generic sheet 12).

Example for Reception objectives

❏ Play the game with lots of cube 'trains' 1–10 or 1–20. The children have to find two trains that have a difference of 1, 2, 3 and so on. (For three or four children you need two sets of 1–10 trains.)
❏ Make a 'staircase' with cube 'trains' where the trains are put in order of length and have a difference of 1 when compared with their neighbour.

❑ When the children are more experienced, play the game as a supervised activity with face-down dotty cards (Generic sheet 15). Again, these are picked up in pairs and the child has to say which number is more (and position them on a number line if you want). Help the children to count the dots and relate that to fingers.

❑ Then develop the game so that face-down cards must be picked up in pairs where one number is one more (or less) than the other number.

Example for Year 2 objectives

❑ Play with a set of 1–20 cards (two sets if four children are playing). Players should find pairs with a difference of 2 at first.

❑ If you use a set of 0–40 cards the game can be to find pairs with a difference of 5 or 10.

Variation

❑ Once the children can find pairs, change the game to finding a small difference by counting up from the smaller number to the larger. Let them choose any two cards and help them to count up. So if 17 and 20 are picked the player could count along a number line, or on their fingers, '18, 19, 20'. Drawing the steps along a blank number line will show up which children when asked to find that difference of 3 would end up saying there is a difference of 4 because they might count the 17 and say '17, 18, 19, 20'. Actually drawing in three single steps or a step of three can prevent this error. You need to note carefully which children make this error. There is often a significant number in the class.

Plenary session

❑ 'Look at my cube train and let's count the cubes. Jez, come and find a cube train that is 2 more than this one. Let's find the numbers on the number line. So we can say that there is a difference of 2 between 9 and 11. Alice, come and draw in hops on the number line from 9 to 11. How many hops of one?'

❑ 'Jake is 7 and his sister is 9. What is the difference in their ages?'

❑ 'Choose a really large number in your head and find a number that is 2 more or less than it. Can you find your numbers on the 100 square?'

❑ 'Do you think you can find differences like this with huge numbers like a thousand or a million? Which number is 2 more than one million?'

Game 7

Octopus game

Addition and subtraction of three numbers

A game for two to six players

Learning objectives

Reception: Add two small numbers.

Year 1: Put the larger number first and count on in ones. Add three numbers.

Year 2: Use knowledge that addition can be done in any order to do mental calculations more efficiently. Add by putting the larger number first.

What you need

- an octopus board for each player (page 25)
- number/fish/dotty cards (Generic sheets 1–4, 5 and 6, 15 and 16)
- spinners or dice (Generic sheets 7–9)
- number lines (Generic sheet 11)
- cubes/counters
- bags for the cards

This game can be played in several different ways to give plenty of experience with mental addition (and subtraction).

How to play

Players need an octopus board each. They generate numbers by taking cards from bags or using dice or spinners, and add the numbers. For example, if the cards 13 and 4 are taken, the number 17 on the game board is covered (if you have written numbers on the boards) or written (if the boards are left blank). The cards must be put back in the right bag. If a number can't be covered (for example, if it is already covered) that player misses a go. The first to cover all their numbers wins.

For a longer game children write the numbers on the game board as they make them and then, once all the tentacles are filled in, they can carry on playing, this time trying to cross out all the numbers they made. The winner is first to cross out all their numbers. If you can stand it, the first to cover all their numbers can shout 'octopus'! An alternative is play the game by subtracting the numbers.

Notes for the teacher

You can choose to write the numbers on the boards before play starts. These must relate to the number cards you are using. For example, with the cards 11–15 and 2–7 you will need numbers on the tentacles from 11+2 to 15+7. Depending on the cards you use, sometimes you might need to repeat numbers on the board and at other times with a wide range of possible numbers to make you might only be able to write a selection on the tentacles. (To make different coloured cards photocopy the sheets onto thin, coloured card.) When you want to practice putting the larger number first, it is important to have the larger numbers in a separate bag.

Introducing the game

- ❏ Say to the children *'Today you are going to learn to add by putting the larger number first then counting on in 1s' (Y1). You take one blue card (larger number) from the bag and then you take a red card (such as 3–7) and you add them by putting the larger number in your head, then counting on.'* (Count on in 1s both on fingers and on a number line.) *'So if you pick 11 and 4 you can cover 15 with your cube.'*
- ❏ Go over mental addition or counting on fingers or with cubes many times before the game is played independently. Make sure all the children understand what is meant by 'the larger number'. You could illustrate this on a number line; all the blue numbers (15–21) are at one end of the line and the red numbers at the left hand (smaller) end.

Example for Reception objectives

❑ You will need to have an adult supervising the game. Prepare suitable cards; for example, with the numbers 1–5 on blue card and 2–6 on red, or use dotty cards in which case children count the dots. Prepare the game boards with appropriate numbers for your cards, such as 3–11. The children could share a game board and cover one octopus each. By the summer term you might find some children could play the Year 1 game.

Example for Year 1 objectives

❑ Prepare number cards, such as larger numbers 12–19 and smaller numbers such as 3–7. The children take one of each and decide which is the larger number, then put that number in their head and count on; for example, 13 add 6 is 19. They write 19 on one of the tentacles. (They could record the calculation as well, perhaps on a number line.) An alternative is to laminate the game board and write on the numbers in washable pen. Players cover the numbers they make with a counter. First to cover all their numbers wins.

❑ You might want to add in the rule that if players think that another player hasn't added by putting the larger number first, they miss that go. But be ready to step in if there are disputes!

❑ To add three numbers you just need an extra pile of cards (or dice). At first it might be best not to use any large numbers, but just use three sets of the numbers 1–5.

Example for Year 2 objectives

❑ Play the game as for the Year 1 objectives, putting the larger number first. Then move on to using even large numbers plus two smaller numbers, for example, 27+3+2.

❑ In the summer term give experience of adding two two-digit numbers; for example, adding the numbers from 21–25 to 12–19. As there are rather a lot of possible numbers that can be made, this game works well with children writing the numbers they make on blank tentacles and then continuing to play by crossing them out as they make them a second time. This can be quite a slow game so children could share a board, one octopus each.

❑ You could have a checker in each group who has a calculator, but encourage the children to see the patterns in the numbers.

Variations

❑ For a different game with adding two two-digit numbers, write the numbers on the tentacles first but place the number cards face up. Children must pick a tentacle number then decide which two number cards they need to take. This is harder than it sounds!

❑ You can play an addition and subtraction game with two 1–6 dice, putting the possible addition and subtraction facts onto the octopus. There are 15 possible numbers, 2–12 for addition and 0–5 for subtraction, so you need one extra digit; for example, a 1 to make 16 numbers, enough for each tentacle. The children throw both dice and either add or subtract to try to make a number they haven't yet covered on their octopus.

Plenary session

❑ *Which is the larger number out of 4 and 16? So which one would we put in our head when we are adding?'*

❑ *Why am I teaching you to add the larger number first?'*

❑ *When adding 17 and 5, would you count from 1 to 17 on your fingers then add 5? If you wouldn't do that, what would you do?'*

❑ *Would you put the larger number in your head if you were adding 5 and 6? Or would you use another method? Why?'*

❑ *You were adding 2 (3) numbers today. Do you think that you can add more numbers in just the same way? So can you add 3 (4/5) numbers together?'*

Game boards

Game 8

Race and pick up

Mental addition of small numbers and the language of addition (and subtraction)

A game for two to four players

Learning objectives

Reception: Use vocabulary involved in + and –.
Count objects reliably to 5/10/20.
Year 1: Understand the operation of addition.
Begin to recognise that more than two numbers can be added.
Begin to bridge through 10 and 20.
Year 2: Mental addition of small numbers.
Adding the larger number first
Bridge through 10 and 20.

What you need

- counters (Generic sheet 18 or 19)
- cubes/teddies/shells
- a 1–6 dice or spinner 3 on Generic sheet 7
- a game board for each group (page 28)
- sticky tack

This game can be adapted to any numbers to suit your children and the 'blank' board can be used in a range of different ways; for example, to include subtraction or as a board for any kind of race game.

How to play

The aim of the game is to go once or twice right round the track adding or subtracting as instructed, keeping a running total (so the numbers could get quite large). They use the language of addition (or subtraction) as the game goes along. Players take turns to throw a dice or spin a spinner and move that number of spaces around the track. If they land on a shape that contains an instruction, they must do what it says. For example, triangles might have written on them 'pick up 2' and squares might say 'put back 1'. The players must pick up or put back that many counters, adding them to or taking them from their winnings, saying what they are doing. *'I had 3 shells and now I have 2 more so that means I have 5 altogether.'* As they get more used to the game you can say that if a player doesn't say their adding sentence correctly, they miss that go and win nothing.

Notes for the teacher

Decide what the different shapes represent for your game according to the achievement of your children. For example, triangles could mean 'add 6' and squares could mean 'add 3'. Write on the boards accordingly. Alternatively, just write numbers on the board, for example a 1 in each triangle. This might be more suitable for the Reception game. There is space on the start to add a number that everyone will start with.

Introducing the game

❑ *'Today you are going to be doing some adding and we are going to think very hard about it because the numbers might get quite large. We will be using lots of the words for adding. Let's write some of those words on the board – someone tell me a word that we use when we add.'*
❑ *'Hold up three fingers. Now hold up one more. How many altogether? So we say that three plus one makes four'.*
❑ Make a large copy of the game and play it with children divided into two groups. Use counters stuck onto the game with sticky tack.

Example for Reception objectives

❑ You could decide that the triangles mean pick up one teddy. Use a dotty dice so that each player has to move one space for each dot on the dice. You might want to write a '1' in each triangle or put one dot. (You will need to supervise the game at first.) Players throw the dice, count along that many spaces and either stay there or do what the shape tells them to do.

❏ Encourage them to check each other's number sentence. *Did Clive say that correctly? What word did he use for adding?*

❏ You might find it helpful to use the words on Generic sheet 14, gradually adding new words as the children get older. You might want to start off with each child already having one cube to avoid awkward sentences with zero – but use zero before the end of the year!

❏ As the game goes along help the children to compare their counters. If you have used cubes they can compare their lengths of cube 'trains': *'My train is longer than yours. I've got more than you.' 'You have 2 less than me.'*

❏ As the children count their counters use it as an opportunity to see who is counting accurately with one-to-one correspondence.

Example for Year 1 objectives

❏ You could prepare the board with a triangle meaning 'pick up 2' and a square meaning 'pick up 1'. Encourage the children to add as they go along, putting the larger number first in their head. For example, if they already have 6 counters and land on a 'pick up 2', they should put the 6 in their head and add the 2 to it. To help them to begin to record addition, you could record for them first to demonstrate that more than two numbers can be added and to show how to use the + and = signs.

❏ Play round the track two or three times or as a race to 20 to give practice in bridging through 10 or more. They can use any sensible strategy.

❏ For a game that focuses on place value, you can mark the triangles with 'add 10' and the squares with 'add 1'.

Example for Year 2 objectives

❏ Write 5 in each triangle and 2 in each square and play going round the track until time is up so that the numbers get quite large. (They will be bridging through 10 and 20.) Remind children to put the larger number in their head first, but to look carefully at the numbers. So if they already have 6 counters and they land on 5, they can choose how to add those numbers together, such as near doubles. They could record each calculation. Remind them that each player must say their adding sentence correctly or they miss that go.

Variations

❏ The track can be used by children to make up their own game. They can write rules using the blank game rules sheet on page 96.

❏ The game can be used to include subtraction as well. For example, players start with 10 counters, they pick up 10 on each triangle, and have to put back 5 if they land on a square. The language of this game can get quite complex so you need to supervise it at first or play it a few times with the whole class.

Plenary session

❏ *Tell me one of the words for adding that you used in your game. Was Sam right to use that word? What other words could you use?*

❏ *'On your calculator, find the key that is used for addition. What does the addition sign look like? Now find the equals sign. Key in 3 + 1 = and tell me the answer. Who pressed the right keys?'*

❏ *Watch me as I count these teddies into this box. How many have I put in? Now I'm going to add one more. How many now?*

❏ *How many is 5 add 6? How did you do that in your head? What other way could you have done it?*

❏ *If I wanted to add 3, 2 and 13, what different ways of adding could we use?*

❏ *If we want to add a small number like 2 to a larger number like 15, what can we do to make it easier?*

❏ *If the answer is 16, which numbers could I be adding?*

Game board

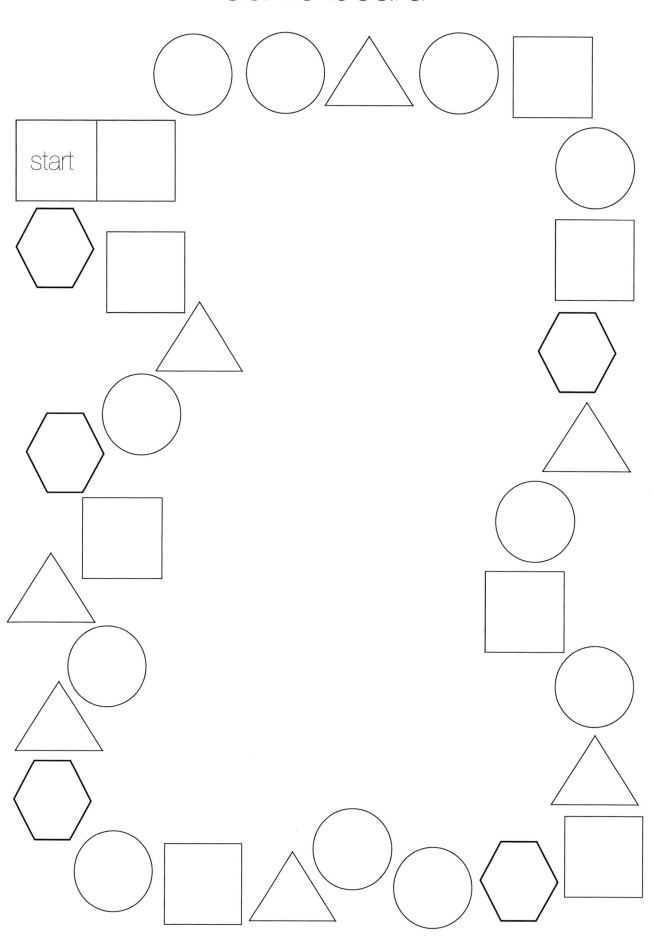

Game 9

Adding five and a bit

Partitioning into 5 and a bit

A game for two to four players

Learning objectives

Reception: Conservation of number.
Not counting from one each time.
Year 1: Begin to partition into 5 and a bit.
Year 2: Partition into 5 and a bit.

What you need

- dotty cards (Generic sheets 15 and 16)
- number cards (Generic sheet 1)
- counters for winnings (Generic sheet 18 or 19)
- cube 'trains' of 5 in red and 6–9 in blue
- two bags

> This game needs supervision at first as the partitioning into 5 and a bit can take a while to establish.

How to play

Put the dotty cards into two piles or bags. Players take turns to take two cards, one from each bag, such as 5 and 7. The player must say what they are doing to add them and how they are going to partition them; for example, *'I've got 5 and another 7 so that is 5 add 5 add 2 so that is 12 altogether.'* If they are correct the player wins a counter and puts the two cards back. Encourage them to check each other and use cubes or fingers or number lines to support the game.

Introducing the game

❏ *'Today we are going to play a game where you have to split numbers into 5 and a bit more. Look at my 8 fingers. I have 5 on this hand and 3 on the other hand. You copy me. Now let's make 9, 5 on one hand and 4 on the other.'*

❏ Write the following pattern on the board:

$$5 + 6 = 5 + 5 + 1$$
$$5 + 7 = 5 + 5 + 2$$
$$5 + 8 = 5 + 5 + 3$$
$$5 + 9 = 5 + 5 + 4$$

❏ Make the point that we split into 5 and a bit like this because it makes the adding easier. However, some children find the concept difficult and you might want to keep this to a whole class finger or cube 'train' game until they have grasped the concept. If 5 is always represented by 5 red cubes and the 'bits' by blue cubes, it can be clearer to show how the two red five 'trains' join to make a red 'ten train'.

❏ For Year 2 extend the pattern by asking a child to come and stand next to you holding up 10 of her fingers as well as yours so that you can show the 'teen' numbers in fingers.

$$15 + 6 = 15 + 5 + 1$$
$$15 + 7 = 15 + 5 + 2 \text{ and so on, and}$$
$$16 + 6 = 15 + 1 + 5 + 1 \text{ and so on.}$$

Example for Reception objectives

❑ Play this as a whole class game with fingers. You hold up five fingers and a few more and the children have to shout out the number of fingers as quickly as they can. Always hold up five fingers on one hand and make the point that they don't need to count those fingers each time because they know there are five. Show them how to put the 5 in their head and count on the fingers on the other hand. This is an activity to do many times as not counting from 1 each time can take a while to establish. Repeat the activity in different contexts; for example, cube 'trains' or strings of beads where the 5 remains a fixed amount.

Example for Year 1 objectives

❑ Play the game with dotty cards; one pile of mostly 5s and just a few 6s and another pile of 3–7. Extend to using 5–7 and 5–9.

Example for Year 2 objectives

❑ Play as above with one pile of cards numbered 5–8 and another pile with cards numbered 6–9. Later move on to using the number cards on Generic sheet 2, using cards 5–9 in one pile and the 'teen' numbers 11–19 in the other.

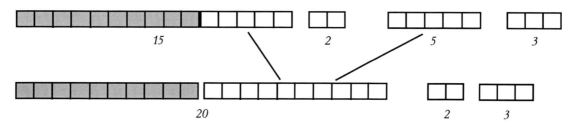

This diagram uses cubes to show $17 + 8 = 15 + 2 + 5 + 3 = 20 + 2 + 3 = 20 + 5 = 25$

Variations

❑ Play a simple adding game taking any two of the dotty cards and adding them. Later use the number cards on Generic sheet 1 and take three of them and add them.

❑ For rules of variations of the game use the blank rules on page 96.

Plenary session

❑ *'Did we need to count these fingers on this hand? We counted them last time and there were 5 so I think there will still be 5. Let's see. Yes, there are still 5. There will always be 5 when I hold up all the fingers on this hand. Let's put 5 in our head and count on to find how many altogether.'*

❑ *'How did you split 7 and 8 into 5 and a bit?'*

❑ *'Nancy had to add 6 and 6. How else could you do that adding as well as 5 and a bit?'* (Doubles.)

❑ *'Show me with these cubes how you split your numbers.'*

❑ *'How did you split 17?'*

❑ *'Why are we learning to do adding like this?'*

Party plates

Understanding addition as the combining of two groups of objects

This is a game that can extend the range of strategies children use for mental addition.

A game for two or more players

Learning objectives

Reception: Understanding addition as combining two groups of objects.
Partitioning.
Year 1: Understanding addition and using the related vocabulary.
Year 2: Adding 9, 10 or 11 (then 19 and 21).
Adding 2 two-digit numbers.

What you need

- a game board of plates for each group (page 33)
- a game board of the party table for each player, pair or group (page 34)
- lots of party food counters (Generic sheet 19) or use cubes
- a recording sheet (Generic sheet 10)
- 1–6 dice or spinners (Generic sheets 7 and 8)
- number cards (Generic sheets 1 to 2)
- gags for cards
- blank number lines (Generic sheet 11)

How to play

Players take turns to throw two dice (later three dice) and put the correct number of cakes (for the cakes, use the little counters on Generic sheet 19 or some cubes) on each plate on Game board 1. So, a throw of 3 and 5 is 3 cakes on one plate and 5 on another. The player must say what they are doing and physically combine the two groups of cakes and put them on the largest plate. If they add correctly (encourage all the children to check each player) one of the items of party food on the table (Game board 2) can be covered with a cube. If players are sharing Game board 2 they need a different colour cube/party food counters each. The winner is the player with the most counters on the board at the end of the game. On a longer game where each player has their own game boards, the winner is the player who has covered the most food.

Introducing the game

❑ Say to the children *'Today we are going to learn more about adding. What do you already know about adding? Using your fingers show me how to add 3 and 4.'*
❑ Give each child 10 cubes/teddies and ask them to make small sets; for example, 3 and 2 more. Physically do the combining using a range of language for addition.
❑ *'So if you put your 3 teddies and your 4 teddies together you can count them and find you have 7 altogether. Let's do that a different way now. We know that this is a group of 4 so we can put 4 in our head and count on 3 on our fingers 5, 6, 7, so we have 7 when we put them together like that.'*

Example for Reception objectives

❑ Play with small numbers; for example, use Spinners 5 and 6 on Generic sheet 7, or Spinner 5 with a dotty dice. You will need to supervise this at first then put a confident child in each group to check the counting.
❑ You can play with plastic plates from the play house and play dough food, or use the party food counters on Generic sheet 19, but take care with plates with several items on them.

Example for Year 1 objectives

❑ Play as above but gradually start to use larger numbers such as on a 10- or 12-sided dice and Spinner 7 on Generic sheet 8, filling in appropriate numbers for your children, and perhaps even a zero space and make it mean 'miss a go'.

Example for Year 2 objectives

❑ Play as above but you might prefer to use 'base ten' equipment to help the addition or use number lines.

❑ Use a dice or spinner to get the first number, then use Spinner 8 on Generic sheet 8 to add either 10 or 9, or use Spinner 7 and write '+10', '+11', '+9' and 'miss a go'.

❑ When the children are more confident, move on to adding 19 and 21.

❑ To add two-digit numbers, you can generate the numbers with the number cards on Generic sheets 2 and 3 (20–39). Players should take turns to take two cards out of a bag. Providing number lines such as that on Generic sheet 11 is important.

Variations

❑ You can give each child a third 'plate' (a circle of paper) and play the same game adding a third number.

❑ With two piles or bags of number cards you can adapt the game to adding the larger number first, ie number cards above 11 in one bag and cards 1–7 in the other.

❑ Play the game in reverse where a child is given a number and this has to be split into two smaller numbers.

Plenary session

❑ *When you put your two plates of cakes together, is that called adding or taking away?'*

❑ *'Show me on your fingers how you could add 4 and 5 more. Can you tell me another way to add 4 and 5?'*

❑ *'Show me by taking hops along a number line how to add 3 and 2 more. So adding 2 is just like saying "count on 2".'*

❑ *'If I ended up with 10 cakes, tell me what I might have had on each of my two plates. Which other numbers added together make 10?'*

❑ *'If I had 6 on the first plate and I ended up with 9 once I'd added them together, how many were on the second plate?'*

❑ *'You used quite small numbers to put the cakes on the plates, then when you pushed your two lots of cakes together did you end up with a larger number or a smaller number? So when you add on, the number gets larger. Let's try that on the number line. If you start on 15 then you add or count on 3, you get to 18 and 18 is larger than 15. It is 3 larger.'*

❑ *'Tell me what you have learned about adding.'*

Game board 1

Game board 2

MATHS GAMES **ADDITION AND SUBTRACTION – Book 1**

Game 11

Kangaroo jumps

Relating addition to counting on

A game for two to four players

Learning objectives

Reception: Begin to relate addition to counting on.
Year 1: Recording addition as counting on.
Begin to bridge through 10 and 20.
Year 2: Using a number line to bridge through 10 and 20.

What you need

- Game board 1 for Reception (page 37)
- a laminated Game board 2 for each child for the Years 1 and 2 game (page 38)
- kangaroo counters (Generic sheet 18)
- number cards (Generic sheets 1 to 3)
- spinners from Generic sheets 7 and 8
- number lines (Generic sheet 11)

> This game can be used to introduce using a number line for addition.

How to play

This game can be played on either Game board 1 or 2. Players take turns to take a number card and put it on the left-hand kangaroo space on the board or write the number with a washable pen. They spin a spinner to find how many places to jump on and they draw these jumps, telling the group what they are doing. They write the number they end on in the right-hand kangaroo space. If everyone agrees they are right, and they have done the correct number of kangaroo jumps, the player wins a kangaroo counter. If they are wrong or say the wrong number sentence they win nothing. Board 2 can be used for a related race game, see the Year 1 game.

Introducing the game

❏ Say to the children *Today we are going to do some adding. Which words do you know for adding? Today we are going to use the words 'counting on'.*
❏ If the children have not had much number line experience, play the Reception game first (see below) on a floor number track.
❏ Show Years 1 and 2 children how to make hops of 1 along a number line and give each of them time to practise drawing the hops.

Example for Reception objectives

❏ Play the game on a floor number track. (This can just be numbered bits of paper, such as from 1–10, but go to 20 before the end of the year.) Make sure you have something for the zero, such as a big red triangle or the kangaroo's house. Use a large version of Spinner 9 and let the children take turns to be the kangaroo and obey instructions given by the others who are spinning the spinner. So a child takes a card from a set of cards numbered 1–4, stands on that number and is told how many to count on.
❏ Once the children are happy with the idea of counting on, use a larger version of Spinner 7 and write on it 'count on 3' and 'count back 3' to make the game a bit more complex.
❏ Each time encourage them to try to make a number sentence. For example, *'I stood on 3 and I had to count on 2 so I took 2 kangaroo hops and I ended on 5.'* Let them put the addition calculation into a calculator to focus on the + sign. Show them how to do the calculation with fingers and cubes so that the link from counting on to addition is made clear.

Example for Year 1 objectives

❑ Use cards numbered 4–9 and Spinner 1 so that these children will sometimes be bridging through 10. They might need help at first to record their jumps on Game board 1. Some of them might benefit from an enlarged game board. At first they will probably do their jumps in 1s, but some might be ready to move on to longer jumps (see Year 2 below).

❑ Check that the children don't count the number they are on as one jump! Lots of children do.

❑ For a teacher-independent game, use Game board 2 and Spinner 10 marked with 'count on 1', 'count on 2' and 'count on 3'. The fourth space can be marked 'count back 1'. Players have to race to 'home'.

Example for Year 2 objectives

❑ Play as for Year 1 but in the summer term move to larger number, such as number cards 8–19 with Spinner 4 marked with numbers to bridge through both 10 and 20; for example, jump 3, 4, 5, 6, 7, 8.

❑ Help the children to make more efficient jumps on number lines, not always jumping in 1s. For example, for '7 count on 5' show them how to jump 3 to get to 10, then 2 more.

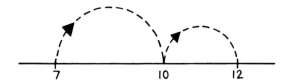

Variations

❑ The game can be adapted for subtraction. For example, using Game board 2, players start at 20 and jump back to the kangaroo. On Game board 1, start with fairly large number cards such as 10–20 and count back the number on the spinner. You might want to white out the 'start' and 'land on' on Game board 1 and reverse them so that the one on the right is the starting number and the one on the left is the number you end up with.

Plenary session

❑ Play the game with children using a large blank number line.

❑ With the youngest children you might want to hold the plenary session around a large floor number track. (This can just be bits of scrap paper on the floor marked 1–10 or 20 and use something such as a blue square for zero.) Help them to describe what they are doing as they count on.

❑ 'Tell me some of the words we can use for adding.'

❑ 'When we were counting on, were we adding or subtracting? So when you count back, is that adding or subtracting?'

❑ 'Sasha, come and draw three counting on jumps of one each on this number line.'

❑ Bridging through 10 and 20 needs plenty of practice at mental maths times for several weeks, for example, 'What is 5 more than 9? How did you work that out? Was there a quicker way? How else could you do it?'

❑ Give children repeated help with recording on a number line to support later addition of two-digit numbers.

Game board 1

start   **land on**

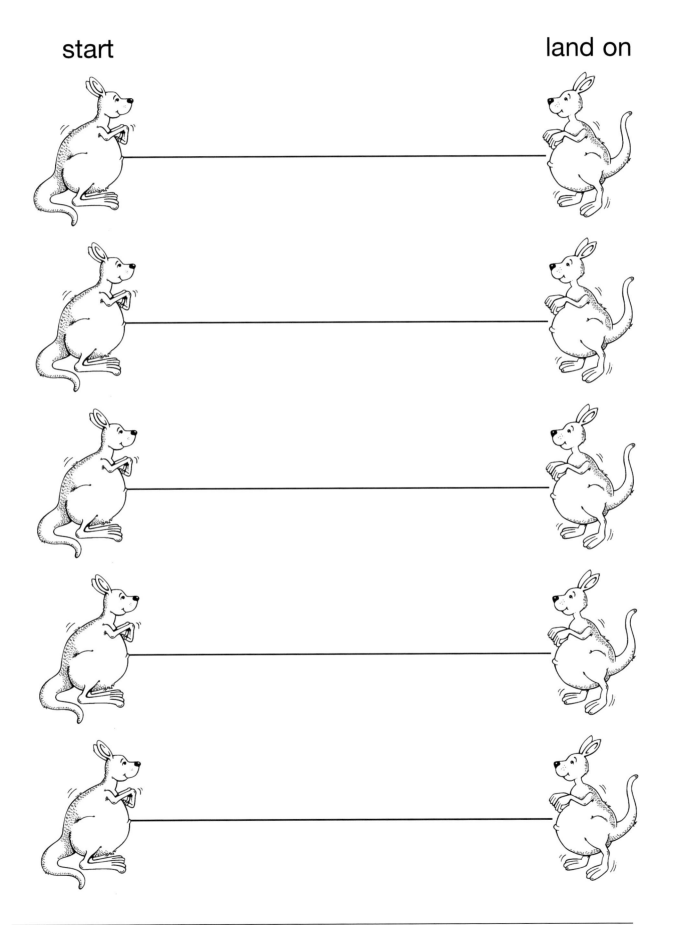

Game board 2

home

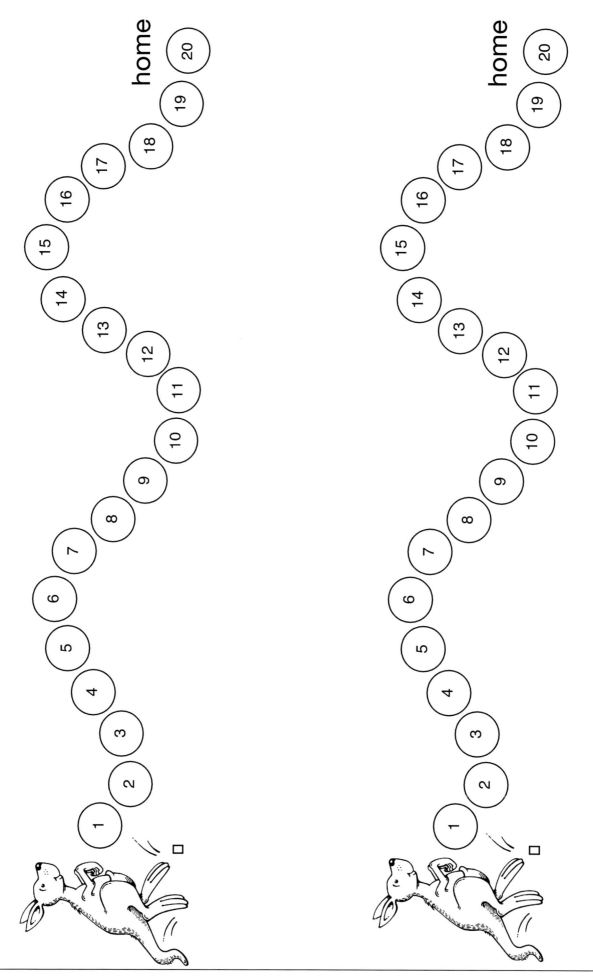

MATHS GAMES **ADDITION AND SUBTRACTION – Book 1**

Parrots

Adding/subtracting tens and adjusting

This game follows on from game 11 developing skills of using a number line.

A game for two players or two pairs

Learning objectives

Reception: Adding two small numbers.
Year 1: Add 9 to single-digit numbers by adding 10 then subtracting 1.
Year 2: Add/subtract 9/11/19/21 by adding 10s and adjusting.

What you need

- Game board 1 or 2 (page 41 or 42)
- spinners/cards/dice (Generic sheets 1 and 6 and 7–9)
- dotty cards (Generic sheets 15 and 16)
- two colours of cubes or two kinds of counters from Generic sheet 18 or 19
- number lines (Generic sheet 11)
- a large 100 square

Notes for the teacher

The two spinners on the board should not be cut out but used on the board as the children play. They can be used as described in the introduction on page 4. Game board 1 is a Year 2 game and Game board 2 can be used for different numbers and also for a subtraction game. If using Game board 2, choose numbers to write on the spinners and then write the related answers randomly spaced on the blank parrots.

How to play

Players generate two numbers with spinners/dice/cards and add (or subtract) them, covering the answer on one of the parrots on the game board with a cube in their colour. The winner has the most cubes on the board at the end of the game.

Introducing the game

❑ *'Today we are going to go over adding 10 to numbers and then we are going to learn to add 9 by adding 10 first. Look at how I can add 10 on the 100 square.'* Demonstrate adding 10 on a number line as well. Make sure the children are completely secure with adding 10 to all single-digit numbers (Y1) and to any number on the 100 square (Y2).

❑ Using a clear number line and a thick pen, demonstrate how to hop back 1 for adding 9 . The Year 1 game is just adding 10 and 9 and it is best to get this established very securely before going on to adding 11.

Example for Year 2 objectives

❑ Game board 1 is set up to do addition and subtraction using 9 and 11, with two players or pairs sharing a board. (You can make other games for this age group on Game board 2.)

❑ Players take turns to spin the spinners, first spinning the paper clip around the left-hand spinner to get the first number and then around the right-hand spinner to see what to do with that number. For example, the left-hand spinner could stop on 17 and the right-hand spinner on –11. The player calculates that the answer is 6, finds a parrot on the game board with that number on it and covers it with their colour counter.

Example for Reception objectives

❑ You can play the game with these children using two dice rather than spinners; one dice marked with 1–6 dots and the other marked 1, 1, 2, 2, 3, 3 in dots or numbers. Use the blank game board and write on the parrots numbers from 2 to 9 in random order. (There will be repeats as there are 25 parrots.) Players throw both dice, add them and find the correct parrot to cover. When they are more experienced you can put some of the dotty cards from Generic sheets 15 and 16 in a bag and they take turns to take two out and add the numbers. (Then put the cards back.) In this case, number the parrots to go with the dotty cards you have selected.

Example for Year 1 objectives

❑ Use Game board 2 and write small numbers on the left-hand spinner, such as 1–10. The right-hand spinner can be marked 'add 9' and 'add 10'. In this case you will need to mark the parrots with 10 to 20 so there will be some repeats. Players spin both spinners and cover their answer.

❑ Another way to play that involves less luck and more strategy is to spin the +9 and +10 spinner first, then choose (not spin) a number from 1–10, covering the answer on the board. This makes it easier to cover a number that is not already covered.

Variations

❑ You can use the blank game board with any spinners or dice you choose.

❑ Challenge the children to make up their own game on the blank board that is both adding and subtracting. They can write their own rules on the blank rules card on page 96.

❑ Selecting (by choosing rather than spinning) a number from the left-hand spinner makes the game have more strategy because you can try to choose a number to cover a parrot that is not yet covered.

Plenary session

❑ *'What did you learn today about adding 2 numbers?'*

❑ *'Tell us how you added 4 and 10. Find 14 on the hundred square. What would be 10 more than 14? What can you tell me about numbers when you add 10 to them on the hundred square?'*

❑ *'Why is adding 9 by adding 10 first a good way to add?'*

❑ *'Which other numbers could you add in this way?'*

❑ *'Do you think this method will work for subtraction?'*

❑ *'Come and draw that addition on a number line.'*

Game board 1

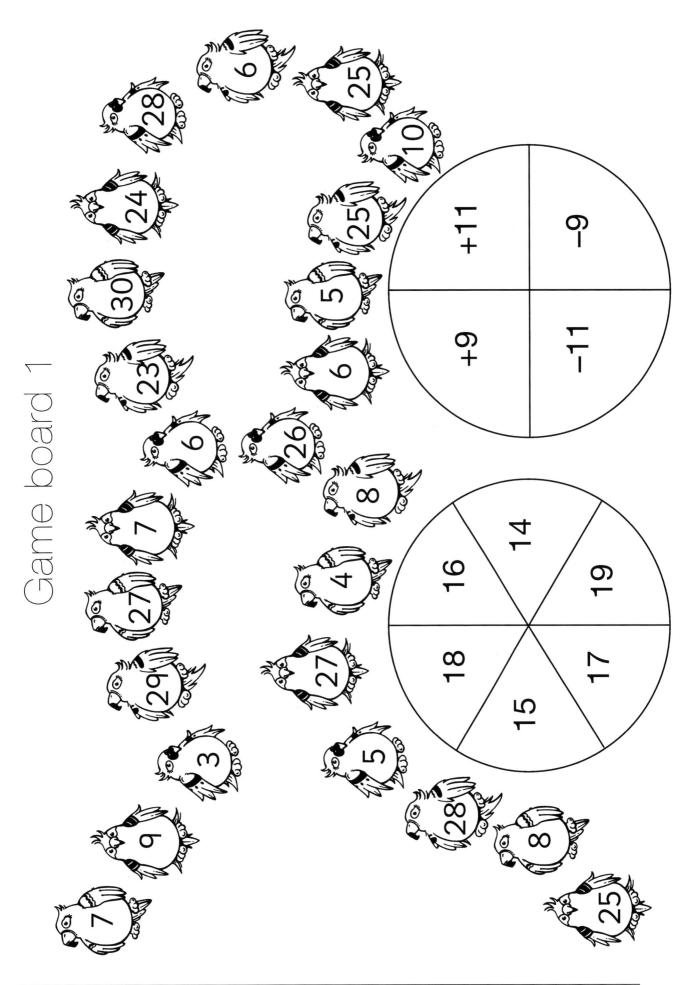

Game board 2

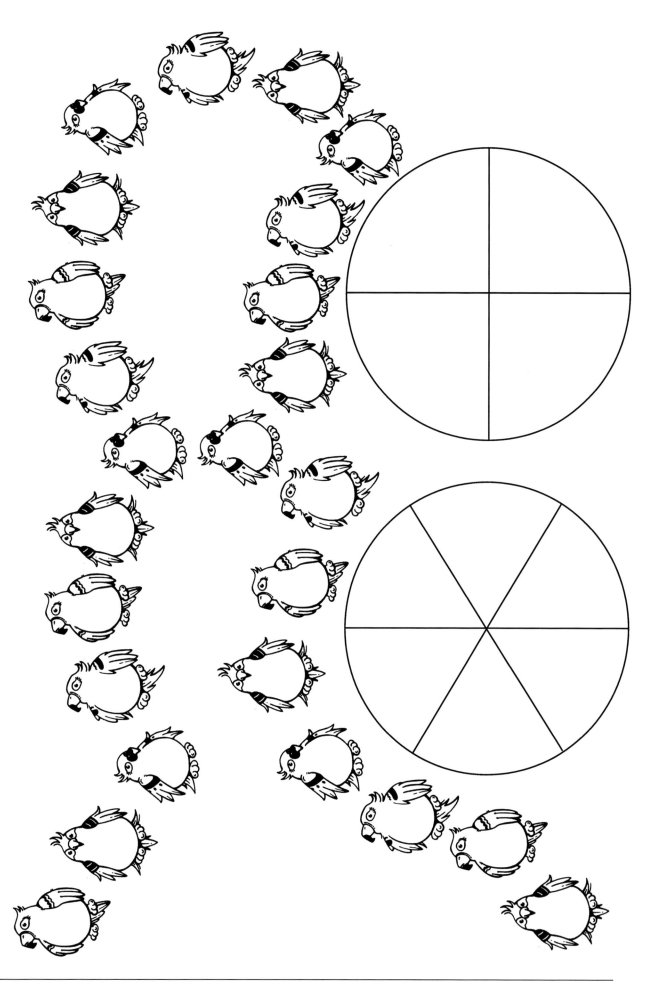

On the bus

Partitioning numbers

A game for two to six players

Learning objectives

Reception: Partitioning objects into two groups. Using the vocabulary of addition and subtraction.

Year 1: Learning by heart all pairs of numbers with a total of 10.
Partitioning objects into two groups.

Year 2: Learning by heart all pairs of numbers with a total of 20.
Partitioning into two or more groups.

What you need

- a bus game board (page 45) enlarged
- cubes/counters/small world people
- number cards (Generic sheet 1)
- a bag for the cards
- counters from Generic sheets 18 and 19 for rewards

> This game can be used for partitioning or adding small numbers, or for number bonds.

How to play

Players need a number to work with, for example 10, or they can take a number card from a pile of cards or bag of cards. In turn, players count out that many small objects, such as cubes or small world people, and tell the rest of the group how they are going to split up their number into people going upstairs in the bus and those going downstairs. They do the splitting saying what they are doing; for example, *I've got number 10 and I'm going to split the people up into 3 going upstairs and 7 going down.'* They place their people on the bus on the game board. If everyone agrees they are right, the player wins a reward. The player with the most rewards wins the game.

Introducing the game

- ❏ *'Today we are going to learn about splitting numbers into two/three groups. Using both your hands, hold up a total of 4/5/6/more fingers. How did you split 4? What is another way you could split 4?'*
- ❏ With a number of cubes suitable for your group, show them how to split a group of cubes into two groups and make up a number sentence for what they have done; for example, *'I had 6 cubes and I split them up into 3 and another 3.'*
- ❏ *'If you put your two groups back together and count them again, what happens?'* (You get back to your first number.)

Example for Reception objectives

- ❏ Put cards numbered from 2 to 10 in a bag. Players take turns, in pairs, to take a number. In their pairs they decide how to split up the number, working with the cubes, counters or small world people, putting some upstairs and some down. They count how many and everyone must check if the total of the two numbers is the number on the card.
- ❏ At the end of each turn the number cards are put back in the bag.
- ❏ When you are able to supervise the group you can bring out more of the language of addition and subtraction.

Example for Year 1 objectives

❏ You can play as for the Reception example or you can say that their number must be 10 each time but they have to find a different way to split up 10 from everyone else. (Keep to no more than four players for this game.) Encourage them to record in their own way (on Generic sheet 10) which pairs of numbers to 10 they have already used. If someone tries to split 10 into a pair already used they miss that turn. There are 11 possible splits. Make it clear that 2 up and 8 down is different from 8 up and 2 down. When all the pairs have been used players can choose another number and start the game again with that many people.

Example for Year 2 objectives

❏ Play as above with cards numbered from 10 to 25, or with pairs of numbers that make 20 each time. You will need to decide when to encourage individuals to work just mentally without objects. You could suggest using number lines for support instead of cubes. Emphasise that if they remember the splits to make 10, they can easily work out the splits to 20. Encourage both recording of the pairs already used and careful checking of the language of addition and subtraction. You can play with the hard rule that if anyone says a number sentence incorrectly, they don't win a reward. (You need to be available to sort out disputes.)

❏ Careful recording will be needed to remember which pairs have already been used.

Variations

❏ You can extend the game by making a 'bus stop' and the target number, such as 20, to be split into three smaller numbers – people upstairs, downstairs and still waiting at the bus stop.

Plenary session

❏ *How many different ways did you find to split 10?*
❏ *Are there more ways to split 20 than there are to split 10?* (Yes.)
❏ *Tell me about any patterns in the numbers.*
❏ *If I had 7/17/27 people, tell me one split into two groups that you could make.*
❏ *If there are 14 upstairs and 5 down, how many people altogether. Make up another number sentence with 14, 5 and 19 with different words.*
❏ *If there are still 7 people at the bus stop, 6 upstairs and 4 downstairs, how many people altogether? How did you work that out?*

Get on, get off

Solving problems with addition and subtraction

A game for two players

Learning objectives

Reception: Using the language of addition and subtraction.
Year 1: Understanding the operation of addition and subtraction.
Year 2: Understanding that subtraction is the inverse of addition.

What you need

- small world people or cubes
- boxes or margarine/yoghurt pots
- Game board 1 or 2 (page 48 or 49)
- a counter for each player or pair (Generic sheet 18 or 19)
- spinners (Generic sheets 7–9)

> This game needs careful supervision at first because doing the addition and subtraction together and developing the language is quite complex.

Notes for the teacher

You need to decide on suitable 'buses' for your children. A small yoghurt pot can be a bus and pieces of drinking straw can be people. Game board 1 is the basic game and is best enlarged so that the 'bus' can fit on. Game board 2 is for later recording in Year 2.

How to play

Photocopy board 1 and cut and stick it to make a long track. Players can cooperate in pairs to play on the same board or they can compete to see who ends up with the most passengers. The game starts by putting a number of people on the first bus. You can either give children the number to start with or they can take a number card. (You don't want to get into negative numbers so at least 3–6 would make a good start. Later they can start with an empty bus so you can talk about zero.) They put the bus on the first bus space on the board. Players spin a spinner to see how many people get off the bus and another spinner to see how many people get on. If a pair are cooperating, they spin one spinner each. They put the cubes on the bus stop in the top half of the circle for the number of people to get on. They put the people they are taking off the bus in the bottom half of the circle of the bus stop. They work out how many people are now on the bus and move along to the next bus stop. Encourage the children to check carefully what they are doing. If they are playing against each other, the winner can be the player with the most people on the bus at the end. If at any time a spin of the spinner will lead to a negative number of people on the bus, they can spin again straight away.

Introducing the game

❏ *'Today we are going to play a game to do both adding and taking away.'* Sit the children in a circle on the floor with a few small world people or cubes each. Pass around a bus (a box or pot), either empty or with about 2 to 6 people on it. At the first bus stop (the first child) some people are put on the bus and the child says a number sentence; for example, 'There were 2 people on the bus and I put 1 more on so now there are 3 people on the bus.' That child passes the bus to the next child who can either take one or more people off the bus, or can put one or more on and says a number sentence. In Years 1 and 2 extend the activity to each child taking one or more off and also putting one or more on the bus.

Example for Reception objectives

❑ If possible, enlarge Game board 1 so that it is big enough to use a margarine pot as the bus. Start with some 'people' on the bus, such as 2. Just let pairs cooperate at first so that they are checking their work very carefully. They can use spinners or take a card for how many get on and throw a dice marked 1, 1, 1, 2, 2, 2 to see how many get off.

❑ You will need to supervise the game at first to make sure the children are using the language of addition and subtraction appropriately. If you wish, you can record numbers on the bus stops.

❑ When the children are used to playing the game, a pair could compete against another pair, but recording numbers needn't be done.

Example for Year 1 objectives

❑ Play as above but once the game is learned, the children don't need to play in pairs, so one child can play against another. Use Spinners 7 and 10 filled in appropriately (remember to use larger numbers on the 'get on' spinner) or extend the numbers by using larger numbers. Again, recording isn't essential but you can move towards it for assessment by the end of the year.

Example for Year 2 objectives

❑ You can play this as in the Year 1 example with larger numbers. For example, start with 10 on the bus, then use a 12- sided dice for numbers getting on and a 1–6 dice for getting off. You might want just to use cubes for people then eventually children have to imagine the people and do the calculations mentally. If they are working mentally, children will need a counter each to show where they are on the bus route.

❑ To record their work they can use Game board 2. Each child needs their own board and a counter and they record the numbers as they go along. If you laminate the boards they can be wiped clean for the next game. Make sure they check each other very carefully. You can bring in the rule that if a player gets their calculation wrong they have to stay at that same bus stop until their next turn.

Variations

❑ Play so that the winner has the least people on the bus at the end.

❑ You can play a target game so that there is an agreed target for the number of people to end up with, for example, 10 people and the player with the closest to 10 wins. Play with a ten- or 12-sided dice (or Spinner 1) and a 1-6 dice. To start the game players agree a target number of passengers to try to end with. They take turns to throw both dice and choose which number they will use for the getting on and which one for the getting off, trying to get as close as they can to the agreed target number to end with. (You can't have a negative number of people! You must leave at least some people on the bus!)

Plenary session

❑ *'When we put people onto the bus, were we adding or subtracting?' 'Which words did you use for subtracting in this game?'*

❑ *'Rosie had 3 people on her bus, at one bus stop, but when she drove her bus away she had 4 people on it. What could her numbers for on and off have been?'*

❑ *'Tammie had 4 on her bus but Mike had 6. What is the difference between 4 and 6?'* Demonstrate differences by getting children to come and stand at the front. Pair them up and the difference is any children left over.

❑ *'Who was closer to the target of 6? Jake had 3 people at the end and Steph had 8.'*

❑ *'Does a number get smaller or larger if you add more to it?'*

❑ *'If you had 4 people and you put 2 on and took 2 off what will your number be then? So what can you tell me about addition and subtraction?'* (One undoes the other.)

Game board 1

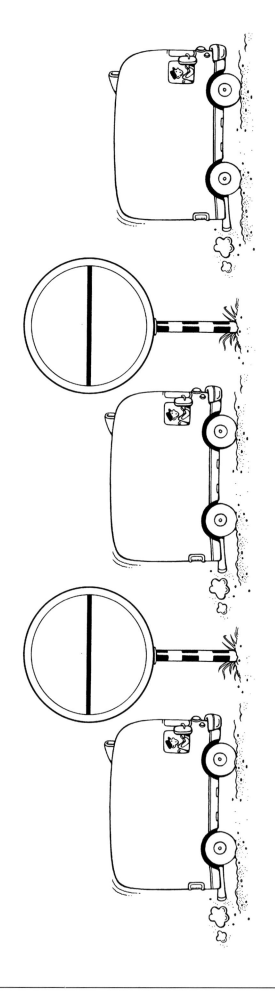
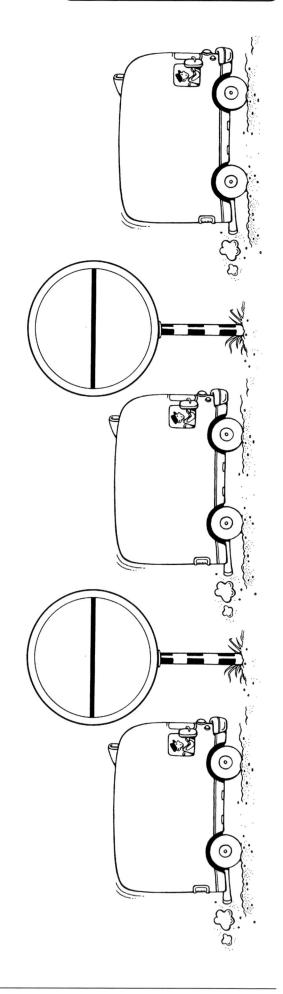

Game board 2

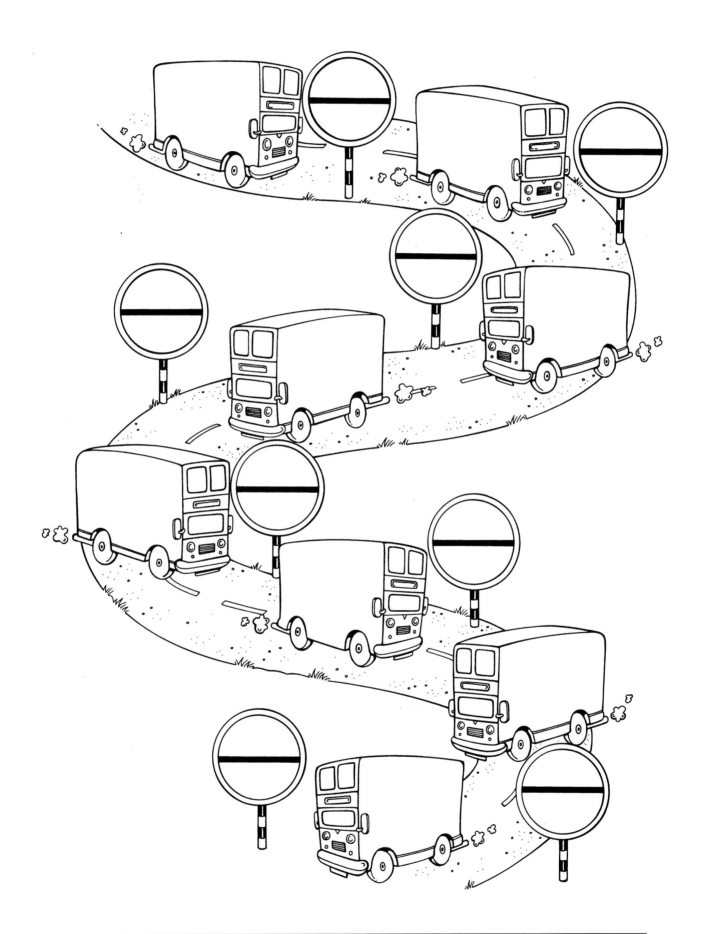

Ten fat sausages

Finding an unknown number

This important game can be played in a range of contexts so that children are making the connections between addition and subtraction mentally.

A game for two to four players

Learning objectives

Reception: Find a total by counting on when one group of objects is hidden.
Year 1: Find an unknown number.
Use the relationship between + and −.
Year 2: Find an unknown number.
Use the relationship between + and −.

What you need

- a game board for each game (page 52)
- 10 or more 'sausages'/ cubes (page 53)
- an 'omelette' (yellow duster or bit of paper)
- a recording sheet (Generic sheet 10)
- counters (Generic sheet 18 or 19)

How to play

Players take turns to put their choice of a number of sausages in the frying pan on the game board. Both players must agree on the number. (Use single sausages at first.) Then, secretly, one player covers some of them with the omelette, leaving a few of the sausages showing. The other player has to count how many are showing and work out how many are hiding under the omelette. That player says how many are hiding. If right, that player wins something such as party food counters or other counters. If wrong they win nothing.

Introducing the game

❏ *Today we are going to think about the symbols we use for addition and subtraction/finding an unknown number in a number sentence.'* Write some calculations and symbols on the board that fit your learning objective and your children, such as:

$$2 + \boxed{} = 6 \qquad \text{or} \qquad 10 = 3 + \boxed{}$$

❏ Emphasise the symbols you want to focus on.
❏ Do some activities with hidden numbers. For example, hold six cubes behind your back. *'6 squirrels are hiding in the tree. One is coming out to find some acorns'* (show one cube). *'How many are still hiding in the tree?'*
❏ Repeat this a few times with different numbers. Use three cubes in Reception at first and build up. Work up to 10 cubes in Year 1 and up to 20 in Year 2.
❏ Demonstrate the game with the paper frying pan and sausages held on the board with sticky tack.

Example for Reception objectives

❏ Play with 3/5/6 sausages at first. Show the children how to use their fingers to work out the number hidden; for example, *'With 6 sausages, if you can see 2, count up, 3, 4, 5, 6 so there are 4 hidden.'* (Watch out for children who count the 2 on their fingers and end up saying there are 5 sausages hidden!)

Example for Year 1 objectives

❏ Play with any number up to 10 at first then up to 20. Play several times with 10 sausages until number bonds to 10 are established, then play with 20, making the links from 10 to 20 clear; ie with 10 if 4 are showing, 6 are hidden; and with 20 if 4 are showing, 16 are hidden.

❏ Play 'ping pong (see the plenary session for Game 1 'Make 10' on page 7).

Example for Year 2 objectives

❏ Give plenty of experience with the teen numbers. For extension work you can use the groups of 10 sausages on page 53 to give experience with larger numbers. You might want these children to record what they have done in their own way using the recording sheet (Generic sheet 10).

Variations

❏ You can vary the context; for example, use 5 or more currant buns and cover them with the baker's hat; or cakes on a plate, or seeds in a flower pot or any other context to fit with the work in your class.

Plenary session

❏ *'There are 10 sausages in this pan and I'm going to cover some of them. Work out how many are hiding. What did you do in your head to work that out? Did you add or subtract or count on or count back? Tell us what you did.'*

❏ Write some of the calculations on the board and show more number sentences with varied missing number symbols.

$$4 + \underset{\text{cat}}{\text{🐱}} = 6$$

Which number goes on the cat?

❏ Remember to show children a range of different number sentences such as:

$$6 = \underset{\text{cat}}{\text{🐱}} + 4$$

$$5 + 1 = \boxed{} + 2$$

$$10 = \bigcirc - 2 \text{ (an extension example)}$$

Game board

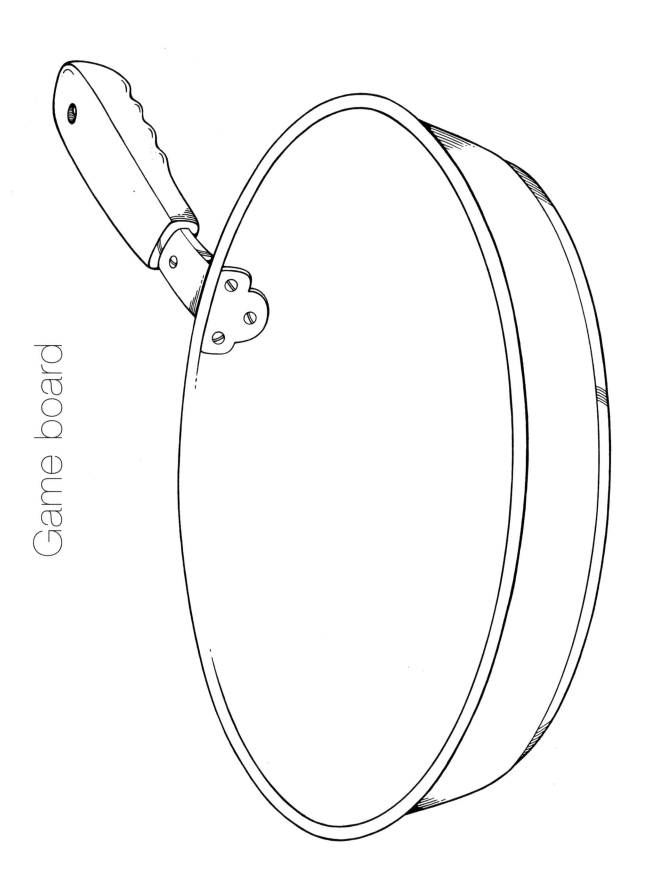

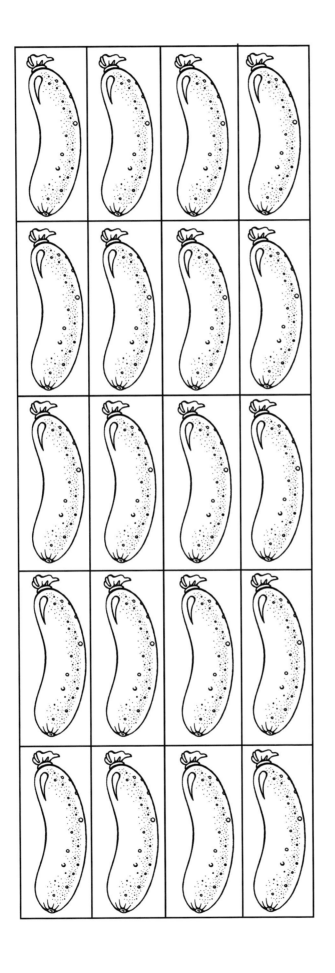

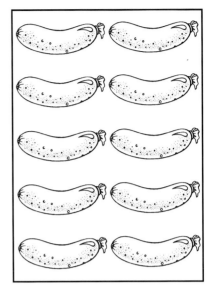

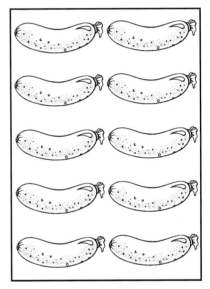

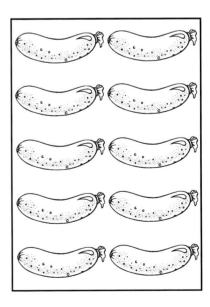

Secret numbers

Find a total by counting when one group of objects is hidden

A game for two players

> This game uses a calculator as a tool for learning to understand how subtraction and addition are related to each other and for solving missing number sentences.

Learning objectives

Reception: Begin to link addition to subtraction.
Year 1: Begin to link addition to subtraction.
Year 2: Starting to record an unknown number.

What you need

- calculators
- a recording sheet (Generic sheet 10)
- counters for winnings (Generic sheet 18 or 19)
- cubes/teddies for calculating
- number cards (Generic sheet 1)

How to play

Pairs of players share a calculator. The first player chooses any number to key in. You might want to give some limits to suit your children, such as numbers up to 10, but remember not to put a ceiling on their work! They can often do far more than we think. Player 1 keys in a number such as 3 and the + key. Player 2 must see this and they both need to remember this number so they can record it if you want, for example, by finding the right number card. Player 2 is given the calculator and secretly keys in another number, presses the = key and hands the calculator back. It might now read '7'. Player 1 works out in any way they want what the secret number was that Player 2 keyed in. If they are right they win a counter. In this example the secret number was 4. Sometimes there are disputes so you need to be nearby, but often problems arise because the wrong keys are pressed.

Introducing the game

❏ *'Today we are going to play a secret number game in pairs. You will have to think very hard about addition and subtraction to play this game.'* Do an introductory activity with the whole class if you have enough calculators or an overhead projector calculator. Start by keying in a number such as 4 then key in +. Show the children how the number 4 stays there, but as soon as another number such as 3 is keyed in, the 4 disappears. Show how to press the = key to get the answer. Ask the children to find a partner and put one of the calculators down as they only need one between two. Play the game in pairs with you leading and choosing some of the numbers.

❏ Explain that as they play sometimes there are problems because someone has pressed the wrong key. If they have a problem it is best to just start that calculation again.

Example for Reception objectives

❏ (Keep a calculator out in play situations and use one in whole class discussions.) Supervise the activity and make up each number sentence with cards and cubes so that the children can read it; for example, *'2 and something makes 4. What is the something? Work it out on your fingers/with cubes.'* (Link this game to the 'ten fat sausages' game on page 50.)

❏ Make sure that all children can 'read' the + and = symbols.

❏ Aim for some children to be able to play the game more or less independently by the summer term.

Example for Year 1 objectives

❏ Play the game using cards numbered from 1 to 10 as the start numbers at first but once children understand the game, let them choose their own numbers. Challenge them to choose starting numbers they can see on the 100 square or number line, but the second child must just put in a number 1–10. (There is no need for children to record what they are doing at this stage.)

Example for Year 2 objectives

❏ The same as for Year 1, but the secret number could be a multiple of 10. If you wish, the children could record what they do in their own way on the recording sheet.

Variations

❏ The game also works with subtraction; ie keying in 6 – to start with. Be ready for negative numbers!

Plenary session

❏ *'How did you work out what the secret number was? Did you add or did you take away? What can you tell me about adding and taking away?'*

❏ *'So sometimes you can work out an addition by taking away and you can work out a taking away by doing adding.'*

❏ The game can work as a whole class game with an overhead projector calculator. One child on the team has to whisper you a number while the other team all shut their eyes.

Game 17

Give me five

Selecting two groups of objects to make a given total

A game for two to four players

Learning objectives

Reception: Selecting two groups of objects to make a given total.
Year 1: Combining two groups to make a given total.
Solving problems with money to 10 then 20 pence.
Year 2: Solving problems with money to 50 then 100 pence.

What you need

- Game board (page 58)
- a 1–6 dice
- coins or cubes
- a recording sheet (Generic sheet 10)
- a number track to 100 (Generic sheet 13)
- counters for winnings (Generic sheets 18 and 19)

> Children come to school having had a wide range of experiences with money, so only use just pennies (or cubes) until you have established which of them can use a wider variety of coins.

Notes for the teacher

You need to prepare the game board to suit your children by writing in amounts in the 'win' spaces. (Don't use 'win 1'.) You will need to enlarge the board if there are more than two players or if you are just playing with pennies (or create more purses off the board). Put cubes or money to suit your children in both of the purses.

How to play

Players take turns to throw the dice and move their counter that many spaces around the track. If they land on a 'win' space they take that amount of money by selecting some coins or cubes from the oval purse and some from the other one. They must not take the amount from only one purse. They show their amount to the other players and if they are right they keep that amount of money and/or win a counter of their choice. If they are wrong they put the money or cubes back in the purses. The winner is the player with the most counters/money at the end. You need to give plenty of time for adding up the money, so when time is short winning counters/cubes is easier to organise.

Introducing the game

❑ With the children sitting in a circle, put two hoops or large pieces of paper in the middle and place some cubes/shapes/large coins in each.
❑ Say *'Today we are going to play a (money) game where you are given a number such as 10 and you have to pick up enough cubes (coins) to make that amount. So if you had to make 10, you could pick up 5 from this hoop and 5 from that hoop. How else could you pick up 10? Show that on your fingers.'*
❑ Ask a confident child to pick up 10 in another way. With older children you might want to write a number sentence on the board: $10 = 1 + 9$
❑ Use a wide range of language to extend the game. *'I have 30 pence. How much more do I need to add to get to 80 pence?'* and *'I'll give you 40 pence. Pick up enough to make 90 pence.'*

Example for Reception objectives

❏ Do a supervised activity where you ask children to 'give me 5' (or whatever number you choose) and they have to pick up a total of 5 from two different purses or pots. Then prepare the board with 'win' spaces such as 2, 3, and 4 or to suit your children. Play the game just with pennies in the two purses (don't use 5 pences at first).

❏ As the number of coins won is likely to go beyond the counting skills of some children, you could use the counters on Generic sheets 18 and 19 cut into strips of 10. The children cover the picture counters on their ten strips each time with coins and they could race to be first to fill a 10 strip. Or they can bring their pennies to the plenary session and you can show them how to count in groups of 10.

Example for Year 1 objectives

❏ Prepare the board with 'win' numbers from 6 to 20. You might want to play just with pennies to keep an unsupervised game simple.

❏ If you can supervise the game you could use a mixture of coins, but you will still need plenty of pennies.

❏ When the children are ready they can record what they win and what they took on the recording sheet.

Example for Year 2 objectives

❏ Play as for Year 1. By this stage some of the children might be able to play unsupervised with a range of coins, but some might still need just pennies or cubes. So if 12 pence is on a win space, they can pick that up as two 5p and a 2p.

Variations

❏ You can play the game the other way round. Players start with some money of their own, such as 20 pennies. When they land on a 'win' space that amount of money is paid into one of the purses (or the amount is split between the two purses). First to get rid of all their money is the winner.

❏ You can play without the board where children take turns to challenge each other to take a certain amount of money; for example, 'take 27.' The other child has to work out how to take 27, some from one purse and some from the other (or from 2 pots).

❏ Use the blank rules sheet on page 96 to write rules for variations on the game.

Plenary session

❏ *If I say "Give me 5", how could you do that taking some cubes from this hoop and some from that hoop? How else could you do it?'*

❏ *If I say "Give me 9", how many different ways could you give that to me? So are there more different ways to give me 5 or more ways to give me 9? Why do you think that is?'*

❏ *If I said "Give me 5" but we had 3 hoops, are there more ways to give 5 now?'*

❏ *'Sam, if you had to pick up 12 in total and you took 4 from one purse, how many would you need to take from the second purse? Did you use adding or subtracting in your head to do that? Did anyone work that out a different way?'*

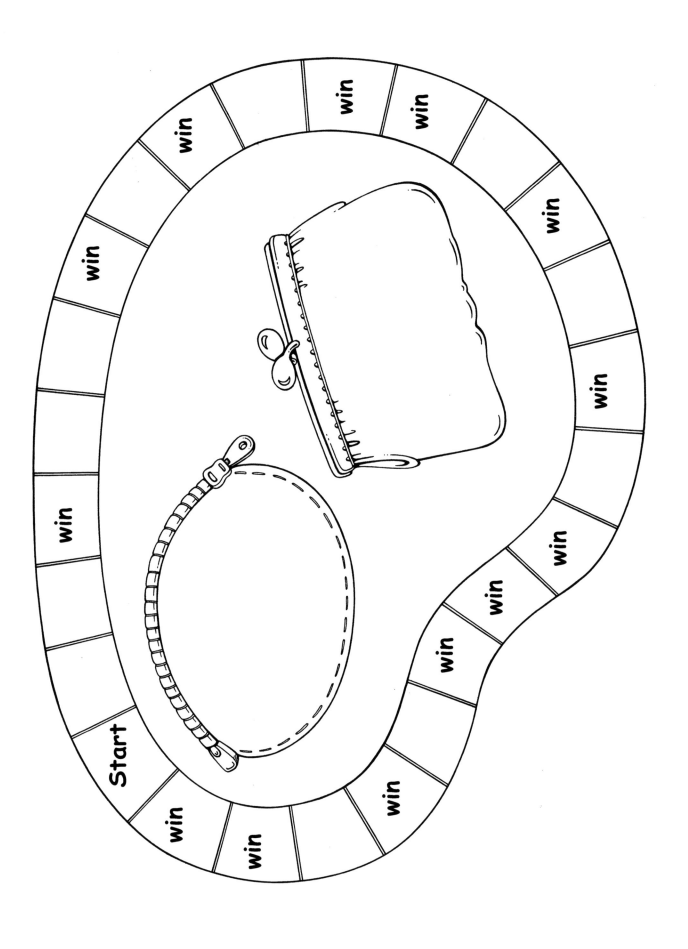

Game 18

Dominoes and doubles

Recognising doubles and near doubles

A game for two players or two teams

Learning objectives

Reception: Learning doubles to 5 and then 6 and above and relating this to counting on.
Year 1: Learning doubles to 5 then 10.
Identifying near doubles.
Year 2: Learning doubles to 10/20, then multiples of 10s.
Identifying near doubles.

What you need

- dotty cards 1–10 (Generic sheet 15 or 16)
- number cards (Generic sheets 1–4)
- counters for winnings (Generic sheets 18 and 19)
- dominoes

> This game can be used to establish what 'a double' means, but can also be extended to a difficult game with large numbers.

How to play

Select a set of number or dotty cards to suit your children. These are placed individually face down on the table and they take it in turns to turn over two cards to see if they are a double (or later, a near double). If they are a double, those cards are kept. If they aren't, the cards are replaced exactly where they came from. The winner is the player with the most pairs of cards at the end.

Introducing the game

- ❏ *'Today we are going to learn about doubles. Look at this domino. It is a double 3. Sam, find another double in these dominoes. So what do we mean by 'a double'?'*
- ❏ *'Hold up double 3 with your fingers, 3 on one hand and 3 on the other.'*
- ❏ *'What is double 2?' 'What is double 5?'*
- ❏ Make sure the children can understand what a double is, then later what a near double is.

Example for Reception objectives

- ❏ You might want to play this with two or three sets of cards numbered from 1 to 5 or 6, with the cards facing up at first. Ask the children to pick out pairs that 'go together' or 'have the same number of dots' or 'look like this domino.'
- ❏ Put the two cards side by side. *'This is double 5. This is 5 and that is 5, so that is double 5 and that makes 10 altogether.'*

Example for Year 1 objectives

- ❏ Play with two sets of dotty cards to 10. You can bring in the rule that, in order to win a pair that has been picked up, the player has to say what the double is, so if double 6 is picked up that player must say that double 6 is 12.
- ❏ Extend the game playing with four sets of cards numbered from 1 to 10, so that a near double can make a pair of cards as well as a double. You can make the rule that a near double is just 1 different from a double, so a near double for 3 can be 3 and 2, or 3 and 4.
- ❏ There is likely to come a point where no more pairs can be found but there are still cards on the table, so count up the pairs that have been made and then start a new game.

Example for Year 2 objectives

❑ These children can play the game as for Year 1 but use cards numbered to 10 and then to 20, or they can use the multiples of 10 on Generic sheet 4. You might also want to add in a '25' card as that is an important double to learn.

❑ For the near doubles, in order to keep the number of cards reasonable, you need to select cards to suit your group, having a number of cards that will fit on the table and according to how many players there are. For near doubles using the multiples of 10 you will need to make cards for 41, 49, 51, 52 and so on.

❑ You can make a really challenging game using any number cards up to 100. You (or the children) need to select them first to keep the game to a reasonable length of time and unless you have a very large table. For example, you might select 75, 76, 77 and 78, but discard all the rest of the cards in the 70s.

❑ Again there are likely to be some cards left on the table that won't make pairs so just start a new game.

Variations

❑ For an easy game with a set of dominoes, put all the dominoes face down. The children have to take turns to turn one over. They keep it if it is a double (or a near double).

Plenary session

❑ 'So what does 'a double' mean?'

❑ 'Show me double 3 on your fingers.'

❑ 'What is double 7?'

❑ 'If I want to add 6 and 7, what might I do in my head?'

❑ 'If you wanted to add 3 and 7, would you use doubles or would you use another method of adding?'

❑ 'Why are we learning doubles? How does it help us?' (To add more quickly.)

❑ 'If my answer is 12, what could be my numbers I was adding?'

❑ 'If my answer is 13, what could be my numbers?'

Game 19

Stars and rockets

Recognising and using symbols

A game for two to four players

Learning objectives

Reception: Recognising numerals and signs + and =.

Year 1: Recognising and using the symbols + and =.

Year 2: Recognising and using the symbols +, − and =.

What you need

- a calculator for each player
- cubes/counters
- Game board 1 or 2 (page 63 or 64)
- dice or number cards (Generic sheet 1) or spinners (Generic sheets 7–9)
- dotty cards (Generic sheet 15)
- empty number lines (Generic sheet 11)

> This game uses a calculator as a learning tool to demonstrate the use of the + and = symbols (and −).

Notes for the teacher

Each child needs a track, so three children could share Game board 1 (you could laminate it) or they could have a game board each. Use number cards to suit your group such as 1 to 5 in Year 1. At first you can write in the start number on each rocket – the same for each child – such as 2. Or (more difficult) each child takes a card (or throws a dice) to see what their starting number is. This can mean that each child starts with a different number. The winner is the player with the lowest or highest number at the end on the last rocket. It is good sometimes to play so that the lower number wins.

How to play

Each player has a start number which they write on their rocket. They take turns either to throw a dice or take a number card and write that number on their first star. (Supervise the start of this game as it can need your input.) The number on the rocket and the star are added together either mentally or on a calculator and the answer put on the next rocket (the planet if using Game board 2). If a player gets it wrong they miss their turn. Play goes on like this, taking turns and writing the number of the dice/card on the stars and the running total on each rocket (or planet on Game board 2). The winner is the player with the lowest or highest number (according to the rules) at the end on the last rocket.

Introducing the game

❏ If you have enough calculators, give one to each child. Make the point that it is very easy to press the wrong key on a calculator so they must check their additions in their head and start again if they press the wrong key.

❏ *'Today we are going to use these keys on the calculator.' (+ and =)*

❏ *'Who already knows what they mean?' (Let children demonstrate.)*

❏ *'Which key means 'makes'?'*

❏ Make a large version of the game and play it with the whole class in two teams.

Example for Reception objectives

❑ At first play this as a supervised activity, with the children taking a dotty card and keying in just that number on the calculator to make the link from counting dots to numerals. Once they are confident with putting in numbers, demonstrate how to use the + and = keys and play the game supervised.

❑ (Let children play with calculators in the play house and other role-play situations as they can learn a great deal from their own exploring of the keys. By the end of the year aim to have them able to key in a simple addition without pressing the wrong keys. Encourage play with larger numbers; for example, *'Key in 100 and add 4'*.)

Example for Year 1 objectives

❑ Play on Game board 1. It is easiest to put in a starting number on each rocket, the same for each child. Play with cards numbered 1 to 10 or a 1–6 or 1–10 dice. Emphasise that players must check each other because it is very easy to press the wrong key.

Example for Year 2 objectives

❑ Play with cards numbered from 5 to 19 or a 12-sided dice or choose a spinner from Generic sheets 7–9.

❑ Once the children are confident, you can extend the game by playing on Game board 2, without using a calculator but doing the additions on a number line.

Variations

❑ Play where each child is given a large starting number, such as 30 or 50, and they have to subtract their card or dice number each time.

❑ Play the game with 10s cards only (10, 20, 30 and so on) on Game board 1 and see who is closest to 100 at the end. On Game board 2 it could be to see who is closest to another target number chosen, such as 400.

❑ Or let the children take 2 single-digit cards in order to make a two-digit number to start with. If the idea is to make the lowest possible total and they have cards 5 and 7 it will be better to start with 57 than 75. You could use Spinner 10 marked +10 +20 +30 +40.

❑ You can also play with a selection of cards up to 100 to add on each time in order to make larger numbers as a starting point for place value and for adding 2 two-digit numbers.

❑ Use the blank rules on page 96 to write alternative rules.

Plenary session

❑ *'Were you able to add 7 to 10 in your head? When did the numbers start to get harder for you to do in your head?'*

❑ *'What kinds of mistakes did you make?'*

❑ *'What is the sign for adding? Make it with your fingers. What is the symbol for equals? Make it with your fingers.' 'What other words can you use instead of equals?'* (Is the same as, or balances, or makes.)

❑ Find finishing numbers on a large wall 100 square and/or number line. *'What is the smallest/largest total anyone made today? What is the difference between Terry's ending number and Sally's number? How did you work that out?'*

Game board 1

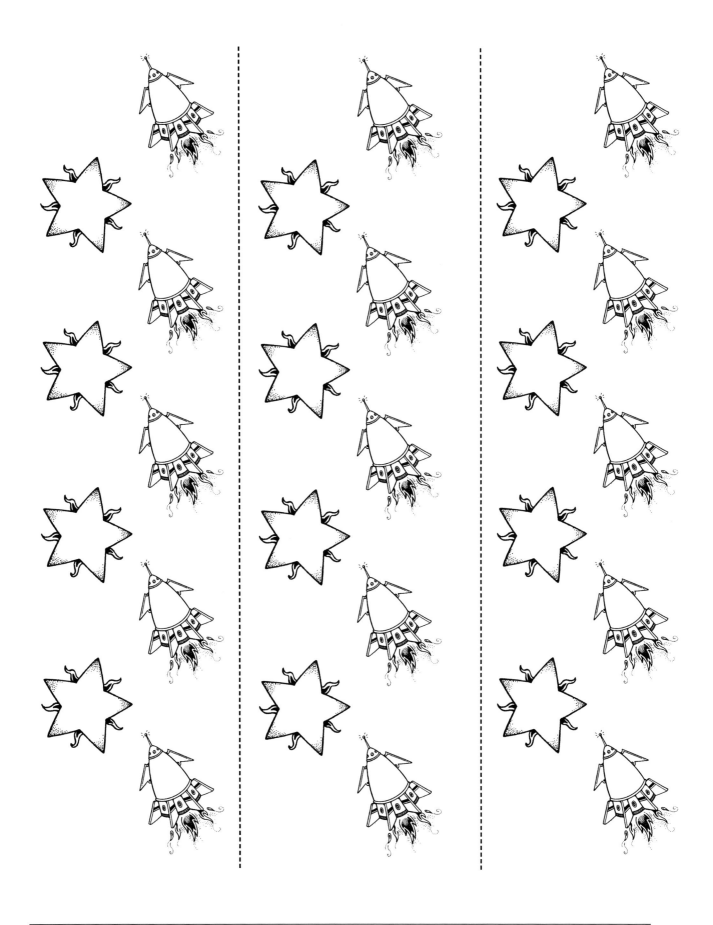

Game board 2

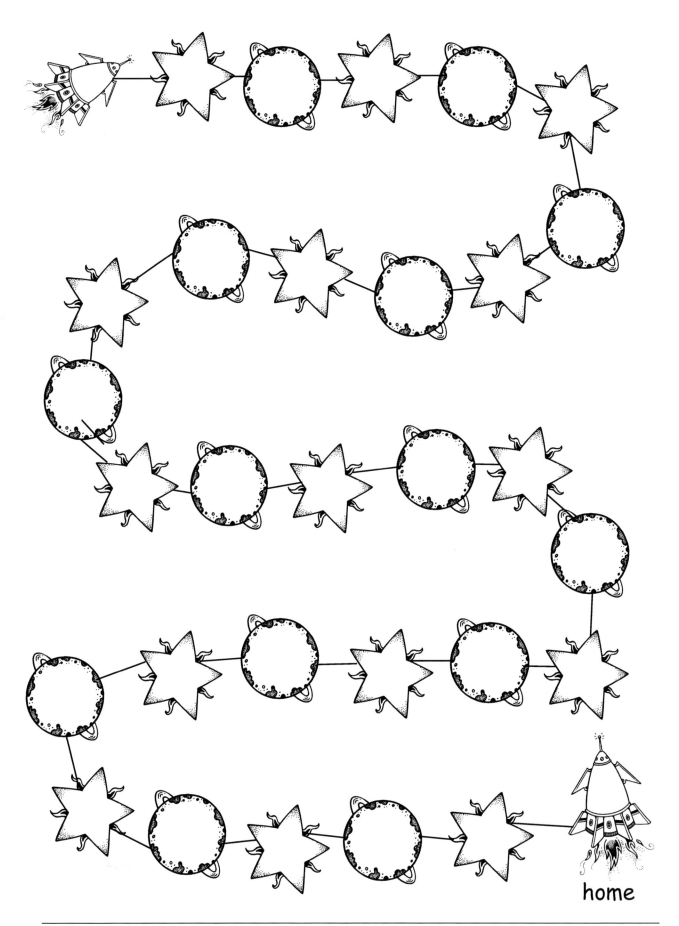

home

Game 20

Score a goal

Consolidation of any learning objectives

A game for two players or two teams

Learning objectives

Reception: Adding and subtracting.
Year 1: Consolidation of adding and subtracting.
Year 2: Consolidation of mental calculation strategies for adding and subtracting. Partitioning into tens and units to add.

What you need

- a game board for each player (Generic sheet 17)
- sport player counters from Generic 19
- dotty cards (Generic sheets 15 to 16)
- spinners (Generic sheets 7 to 9) or make flash cards

This game can be used for a wide range of learning objectives both in maths and literacy.

How to play

Two players or two teams share one game board and decide who is going to shoot into which goal. Each player or team has a counter. These counters are put on the central circle. Two numbers are needed to add together; this can be done with spinners or dice. Alternatively, you could have prepared cards with addition or other calculations on them (for example, '3 + 4' or '12 + 19' or '1 more than 6' or '6 pence add 2 pence'). Players take turns to take a card, spin the spinners or throw the dice and do the calculation. If they get the correct answer they move their counter one space towards the goal. Encourage the children to check very carefully and to ask you or a confident child to help with disputes. If using the calculation cards, you can make the game self checking by writing the answers on the backs of the cards but, in this case, put the pile with the questions facing up. The winner is first to get a goal. You can play the game with two children on each team, each with their own counter; in this case it is the first team to get both counters to the goal. Play another game, the team that lost last time going first. (The player who goes first has an advantage.)

Introducing the game

- ❏ *Today you are going to play a game called score a goal and you will be practising how to add 2 numbers together'* (or whatever concept you want to practise).
- ❏ Do a few examples of the activity you want to practise, for example, show some cards such as '9 add 3 =' and show how you move one space towards the goal if you answer it correctly.

Examples for Reception objectives

- ❏ You could play with the dotty cards and when these are turned over the child counts the dots and says the number. If correct they move one space.
- ❏ For a game to recognise numerals, use cards numbered from 1 to 10 and the children have to say the numbers.
- ❏ With dotty cards 1–10 and number cards 1–10 all face up, the children can find a pair (3 dots and a 3) and if correct move one space.
- ❏ The game will work with many supervised activities; for example, when you ask children to make a cube 'train' of a certain number they move one space towards the goal.

Example for Year 1 objectives

❑ Play the game with flash cards to practise the number bonds suitable for the group; for example, addition facts for all pairs of numbers with a total of up to at least 10. You can generate these numbers using two copies of Spinner 13, both marked 1–5.

❑ For numbers to 12 use two 1–6 dice.

❑ To consolidate subtraction facts you can use two copies of Spinner 13, one marked 6–10 and the other marked 1–5.

Example for Year 2 objective

❑ Play as for Year 1 but extend the numbers. Flash cards can be for +9, +11, –9, –11 and so on, or, in the summer term, addition of two-digit numbers; for example, 15 + 16 and 31 + 26, splitting into tens and units.

❑ You can use cards 10–30 and each time a card is taken, the player must say what the double is. If correct, the player moves one space towards the goal.

❑ A mixture of flash cards can be used to ask the children to choose the best strategy for the numbers (but you need to supervise this).

Variations

❑ Whole class games can be played with the children in two teams and a large copy of the game. The counters on Generic sheet 18 or 19 can be stuck onto the board with sticky tack.

❑ (The game can be played with literacy tasks, for example, read a word or make up another word that rhymes and so on.)

❑ Use the blank rules on page 96 to write alternative rules.

Plenary session

❑ Focus the questions on the learning objective.

❑ *'How did you do that?'*

❑ *'Was it quicker to add 10 then subtract 1 or quicker for you to split those numbers into tens and units?'*

0	1	2
3	4	5
<u>6</u>	7	8
<u>9</u>	10	11
12	13	14

15	16	17
18	19	20
21	22	23
24	25	26
27	28	29

30	31	32
33	34	35
36	37	38
39	40	41
42	43	44

45	46	47
48	49	50
60	70	80
90	100	

MATHS GAMES **ADDITION AND SUBTRACTION – BOOK 1**

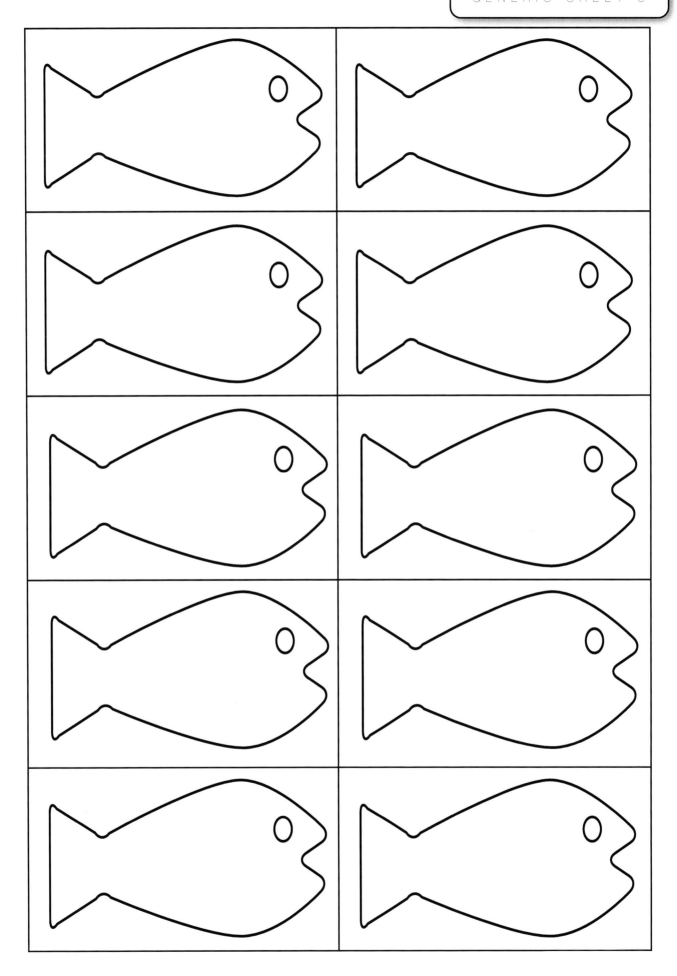

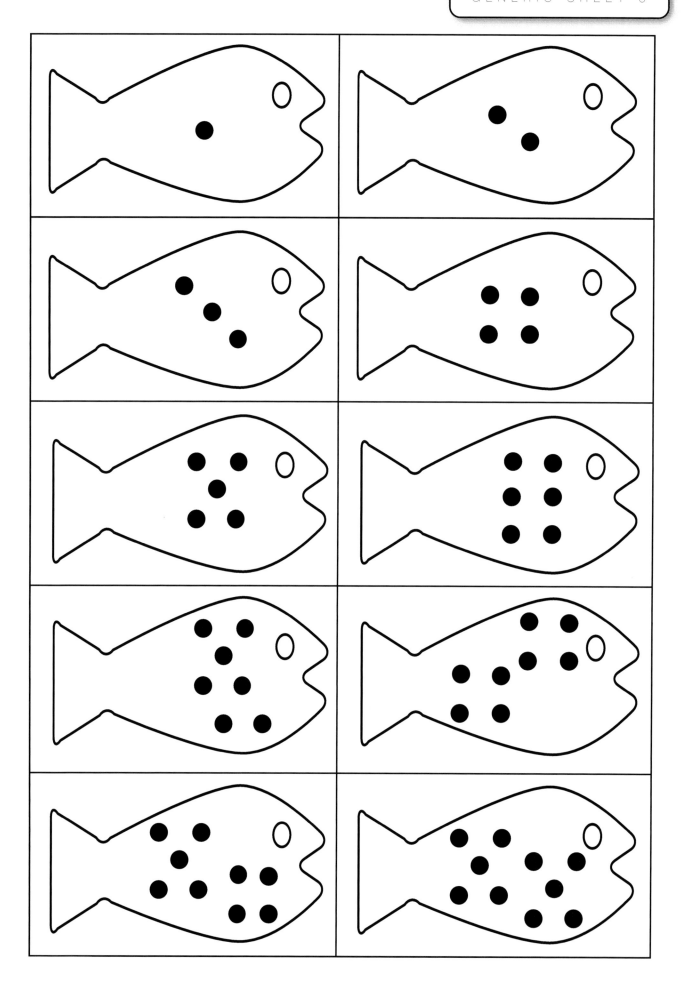

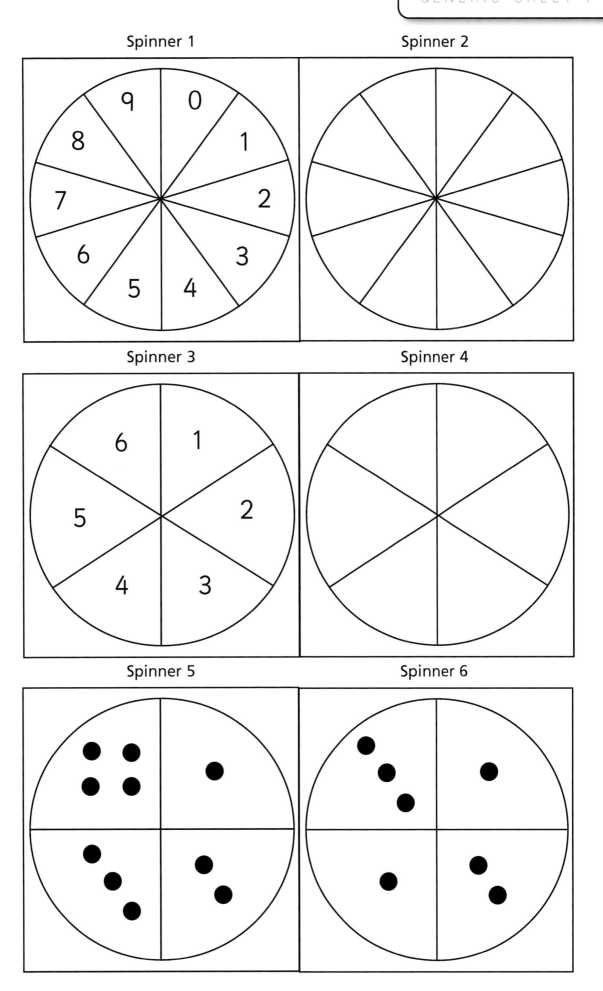

Spinner 1

Spinner 2

Spinner 3

Spinner 4

Spinner 5

Spinner 6

Spinner 7

Spinner 8

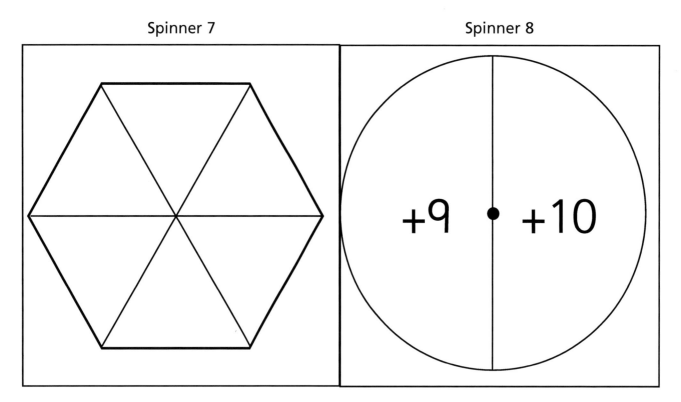

Spinner 9

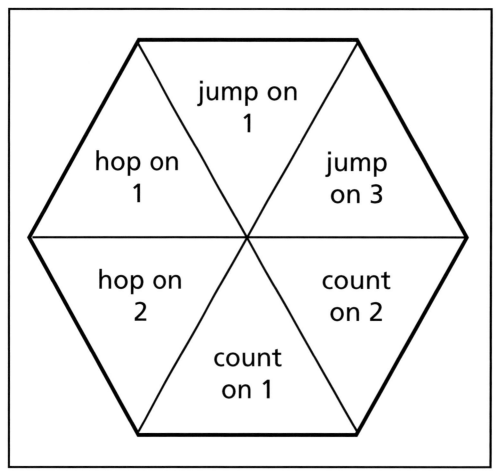

Spinner 10

Spinner 11

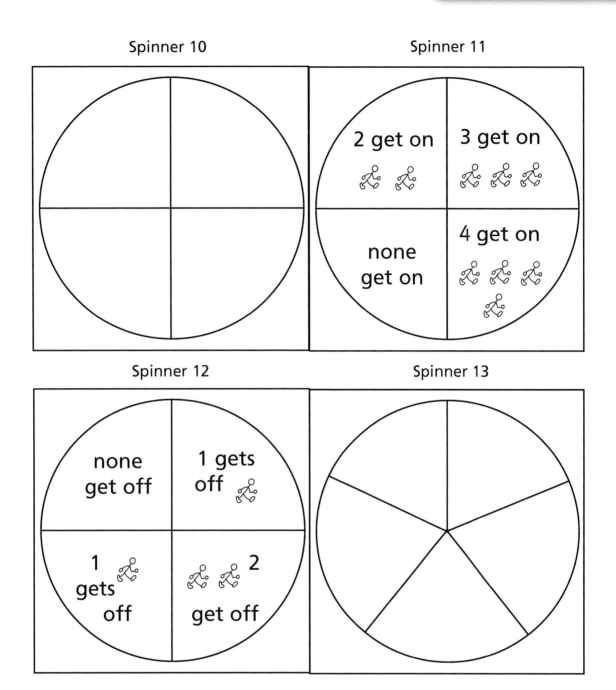

Spinner 12

Spinner 13

Recording sheet

Name: _____ Date: _____

We are playing the game _____

My numbers are:

I learned _____

I was good at _____

_____

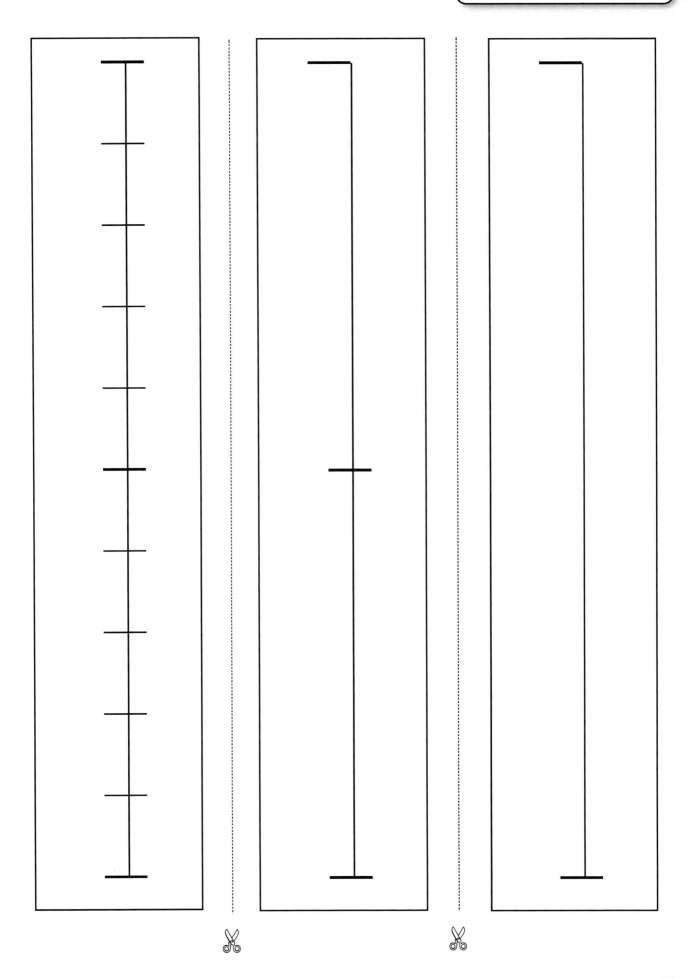

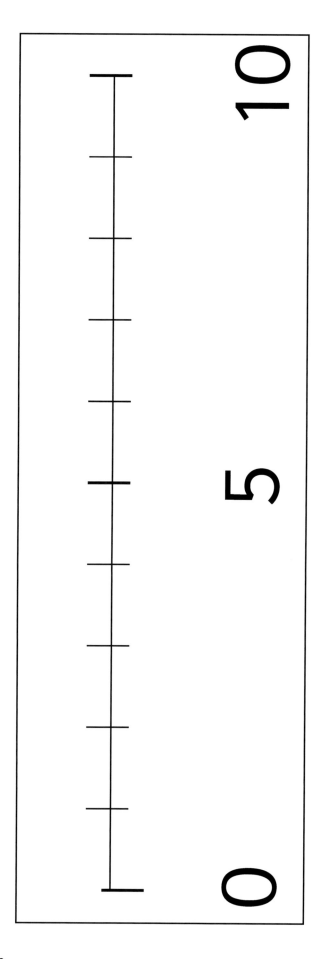

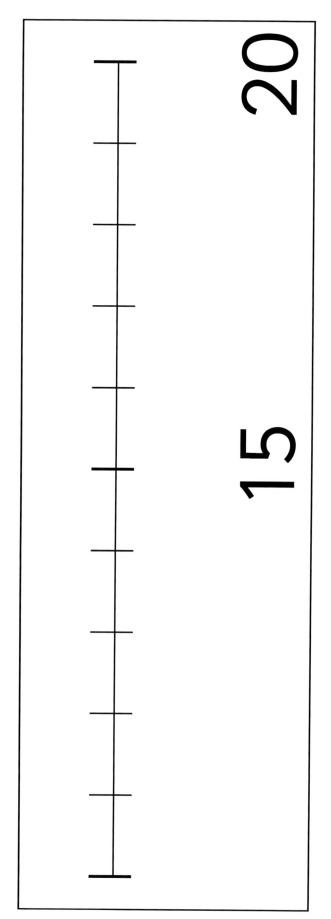

0										
	1	2	3	4	5	6	7	8	9	
										10
	19	18	17	16	15	14	13	12	11	
20										
	21	22	23	24	25	26	27	28	29	
										30
	39	38	37	36	35	34	33	32	31	
40										
	41	42	43	44	45	46	47	48	49	
										50
	59	58	57	56	55	54	53	52	51	
60										
	61	62	63	64	65	66	67	68	69	
										70
	79	78	77	76	75	74	73	72	71	
80										
	81	82	83	84	85	86	87	88	89	
										90
	99	98	97	96	95	94	93	92	91	
100										

count on	difference between	+
count back	altogether makes	—
and	added to	=
add	plus	more
subtract	jump back	less
take away	jump forward	fewer
equals	balances	makes

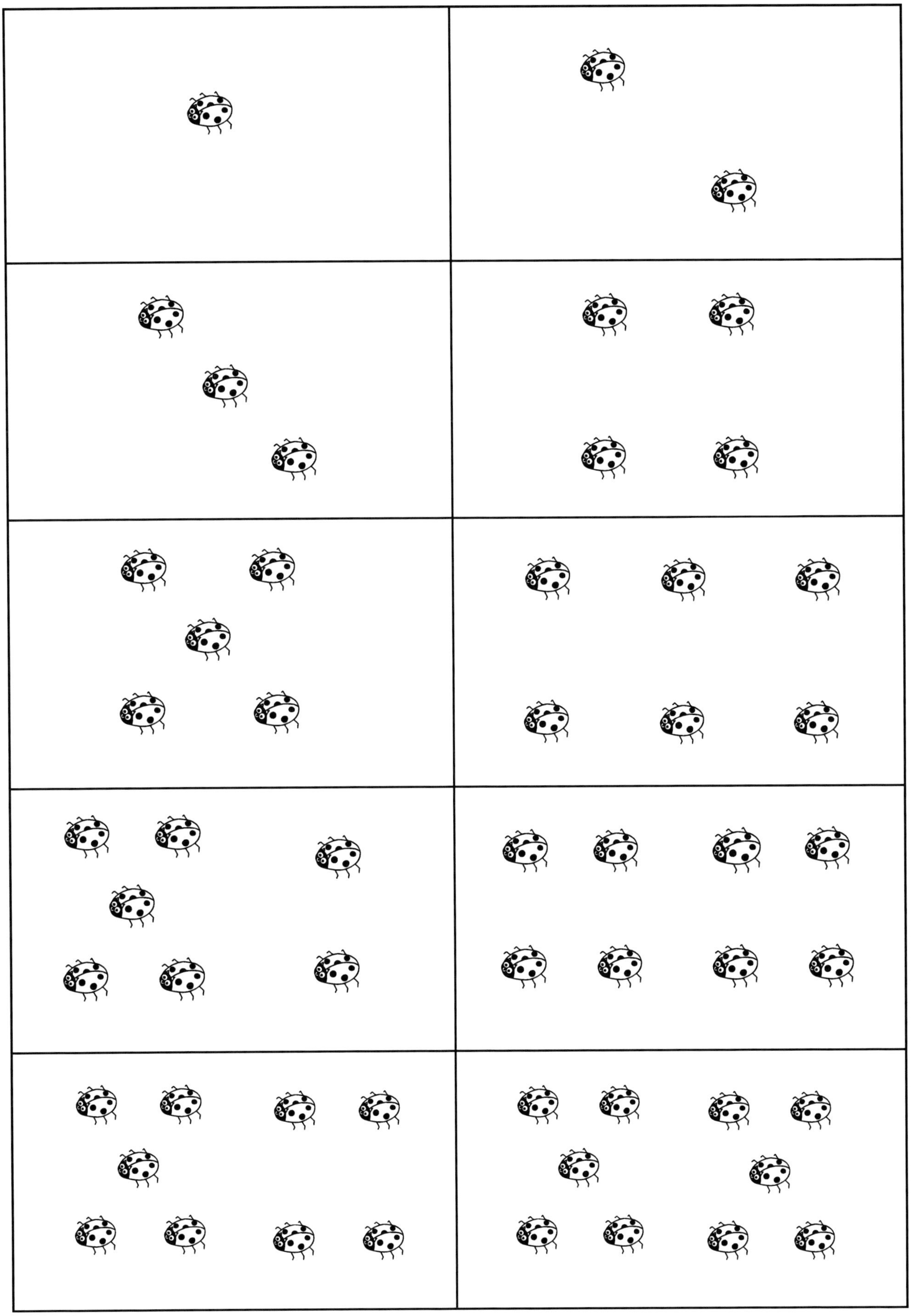

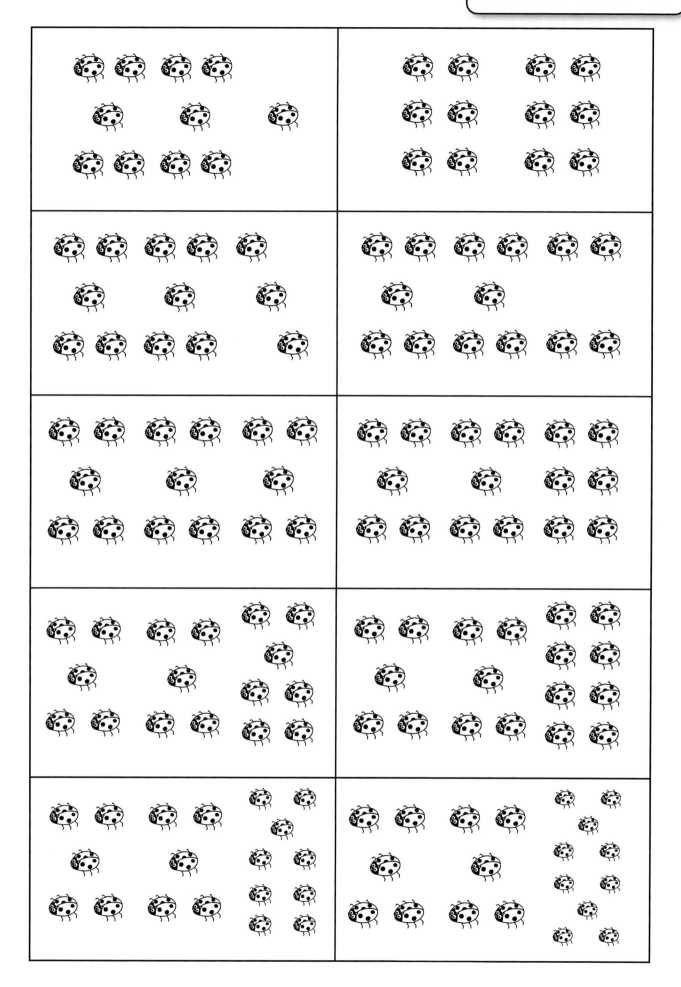

MATHS GAMES **ADDITION AND SUBTRACTION – BOOK 1**

Score a goal

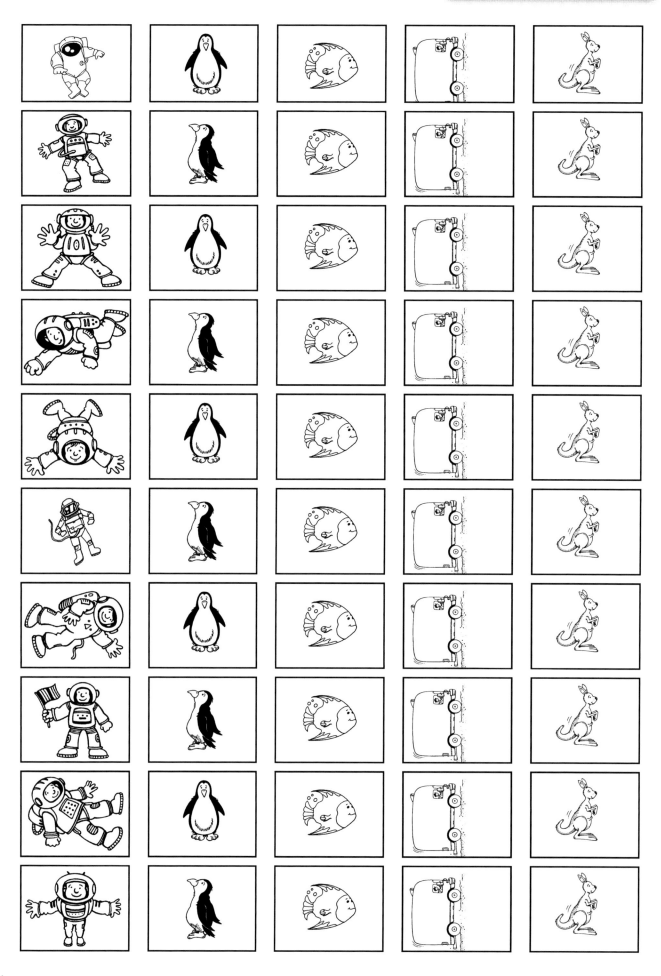

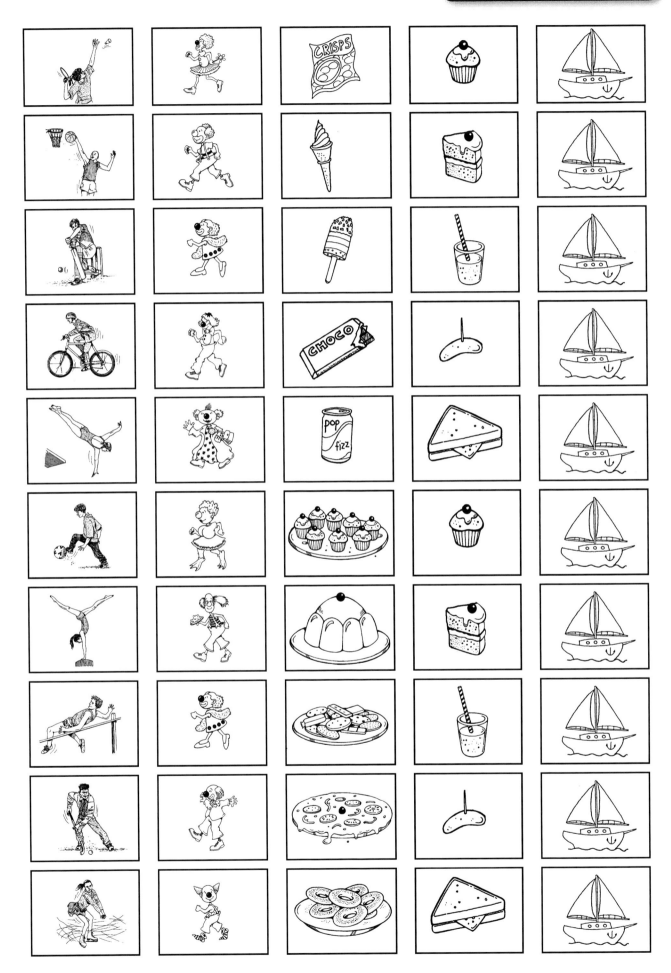

Make 10

A game for two to four players

You will need

- number cards

How to play

- Put the cards on the table, black numbers facing up.

- Take turns to tell the others in your group the number you are going to find; for example, 'I'm going to find red number 3.'

- If you pick up the correct card, you win that card.

Snakey sentences

A game for two to six players

You will need

- pencil
- snake sheet
- snake words

How to play

- Take a snake word in turns.

- Use your snake word to make a sentence. For example, if you pick 'add' you can say '4 add 3 makes 7'.

- If everyone agrees you are right, put 'add' on your first snake.

- Then someone else has a go, but only let them put their word on their first snake if they say their sentence right.

- If you pick a word you already have on one of your snakes you miss that turn.

- Race to get five different words, one on each of your snakes.

Three blind mice

A game for two or more players

You will need:
- blind mice number cards

How to play
- Put the mice number cards face down on the table.

- Take turns to turn over three cards. If they go together (such as 3, 2 and 5, because you can make a sentence with them) you can keep those cards.

- If they don't go together, carefully put all three cards back in exactly the same place.

- The winner has the most sets of three cards at the end.

Something fishy

A game for two or more players

You will need
- fish number cards
- a pond and fishing rod

How to play
- Put the fish in the pond and take turns to fish out two of them.
- Add the numbers on your fish.
- If you are right you win a counter.

Feed the penguins

A game for two to four players

You will need

- a counter each
- a game board
- lots of 'fish'
- a 1–6 dice or spinner

How to play

- Start with a 'train' of cubes 20 long. These are your fish.

- You are going to feed these fish to the penguins and see who has fed them the most fish by the end.

- Take turns to throw the dice and move your counter that many spaces around the penguin pool.

- If you land on a space with some fish on it, feed that many of your fish to the penguins and say how many fish you have left.

- When everyone is back to the start, see who has the fewest fish.

Difference pairs

A game for two to eight players

You will need

- cubes
- number cards
- number lines

How to play

- Decide on the difference number you will play with, such as 'a difference of 2'.

- Put your number cards face down on the table.

- Take turns to turn two of the cards over. If they have a difference of 2 you can keep them. If not, put the cards back in exactly the same place.

- The winner has the most pairs of cards.

Octopus game

A game for two to six players

You will need

- an octopus board
- number cards
- spinners or dice
- counters

How to play

- Take two cards. Decide which is the larger number.

- Put the larger number in your head, such as 17, then count on in 1s to add the smaller number. For example, 17 add 2 is 19.

- Cover 19 with your colour counter.

- Race to be first to cover all your numbers.

Race and pick up

A game for two to four players

You will need

- a counter for each player
- one board
- dice or spinner
- cubes or counters

How to play

- Decide what the shapes mean on the board. For example, a circle could mean 'Pick up 2'.

- Take turns to throw the dice and move that many spaces around the board.

- If you land on a space where you win cubes you must say an adding sentence; for example, 'I had no cubes then I landed on "Pick up 3" so that is zero add 3 makes 3.'

- If you say the sentence correctly you win that many cubes. If you don't say it correctly, you don't win anything.

- The winner has the most cubes at the end of the game.

Adding five and a bit

A game for two to four players

You will need

- number cards
- counters
- cubes

How to play

- Take turns to take two cards, one from each bag.

- Add your two numbers by splitting them into 5 and a bit.

- Tell everyone what you are doing and if they think you did it right you win a cube.

- The player with the most cubes wins.

Party plates

A game for two or more players

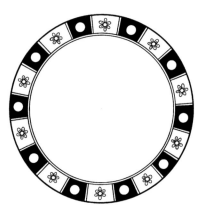

You will need

- a plate game board for each player or each group
- a table game board for each group
- counters, a different colour for each player
- two dice or spinners
- number lines

How to play

- Take turns to throw both dice, such as 2 and 4.

- Put 2 cakes on the first plate and 4 on the second one.

- Now put all the cakes together on the big plate and add the two numbers, using a number line if you want.

- If you are right you win a cube and put that on one of the party foods on the table game board. If you are wrong you win nothing.

- The winner is the player who wins the most food.

Kangaroo jumps

A game for two to four players

You will need

- a game board   • counters   • number cards   • spinner

How to play

- Take turns to take a number card and put it on the kangaroo on the left of your game board.

- Spin the spinner to find how many kangaroo hops to take.

- Tell everyone how many jumps you are going to take, draw these jumps on your game board and write in the number you end on.

- If everyone agrees you did it right, you win a counter.

Parrots

A game for two players or two pairs

You will need

- a game board
- spinners/cards/dice
- cubes/counters in two colours
- number lines

How to play

- Take turns to make two numbers with dice or spinners or cards.

- Add your numbers using a number line.

- If you can, cover a parrot with your answer with one of your colour cubes. If there is no parrot uncovered with your number you miss that go.

- The winner has the most parrots covered at the end.

On the bus

A game for two to six players

You will need

- a game board
- 'people'
- number cards (and bags)
- counters

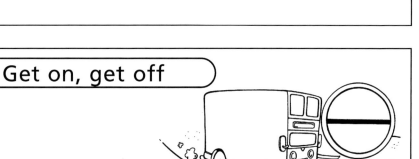

How to play

- Decide on a number that everyone is going to work with, such as 10 or 20, or take a number card to decide how many.
- Everyone counts out that many 'people'. (Or use a number line.)
- Take turns to split your 'people' into two groups, one set upstairs and one set downstairs. Tell everyone what you are doing.
- If you say your splitting correctly, you win a counter.
- Try to win three or more rewards each before it is time to stop.

Get on, get off

A game for two players

You will need

- a game board
- 'people'
- spinners or dice

How to play

- Decide whether the winner will be the person with the fewest or the most people on their bus at the end.

- Put some people on your bus to start with. You can both start with the same number if you want, or throw a dice.

- Take it in turns to spin the 'get on' and the 'get off' spinners. Take those numbers of people on and off your bus and say what you are doing and how many people are left on your bus.

- Keep taking turns like this.

- If someone says their number sentence wrong they don't move on to the next bus stop.

- Watch carefully to check what your partner is doing.

Ten fat sausages

A game for two to four players

You will need

- sausages
- a pan
- a cloth or paper for an omelette
- counters

How to play

- Decide on how many sausages you will play with each time. Both players must know this number.
- One player secretly covers some of the sausages with the omelette.
- The second player looks at the sausages that are showing and has to work out how many are hidden under the omelette.
- If correct, that player wins a counter.
- The player with the most counters at the end wins.

Secret numbers

A game for two players

You will need

- one calculator
- counters

How to play

- Take turns to start with the calculator.
- Player 1 puts a number into the calculator that Player 2 must see. Player 1 presses the + key.
- Player 2 secretly puts in another number, presses the = key and gives the calculator back to Player 1.
- Player 1 must now work out what the secret number was.
- If Player 1 is right, they win a counter.
- See who wins the most counters once time is up.

Give me five

A game for two to four players

You will need

- a board
- coins or cubes
- a dice
- a counter each
- counters for winnings

How to play

- Take turns to throw the dice and move that many spaces around the track.

- If you land on a win space, you must take that many cubes (or that amount of money) but you must take some from one purse and some from the other.

- Show everyone your coins. If you have taken the right amount you keep them, (or win a counter). If you took the wrong amount, put them back!

- See who has the most at the end.

Dominoes and doubles

A game for two players or two teams

You will need

- number cards

How to play

- Put the number cards face down.

- Take turns to find a double or near double.

- If you are right, you keep that pair of cards.

- If you are wrong, put the cards back exactly where they were.

- The winner has the most pairs of cards at the end.

Stars and rockets

A game for two to four players

You will need

- a calculator each
- a game board and pencil
- number cards
- dice or spinners

How to play

- Write a starting number on your first rocket.

- Take turns to take a card and write the number on your first star.

- Add that star number to the number on your first rocket.

- Write that new number on your next rocket.

- The winner has the lowest number on their last rocket.

Score a goal

A game for two players or two teams

You will need

- dice, spinners
- number cards
- or flash cards
- a counter each

How to play

- Take turns to take a flash card and work out the answer.

- If you are right, move one space towards the goal.

- If you are wrong, stay where you are.

- First to get to the goal score one goal!

- Play again, but let the loser start first.

A game for _____ players.

You will need

-
-
-

How to play

-
-
-
-
-

A game for _____ players.

You will need

-
-
-

How to play

-
-
-
-
-